geskes.hack Landschaftsarchitekten (Hg. / Ed.)

IN DEN PARK GEHEN

IN THE PARK

jovis

INHALT / CONTENT

Der Park der Gegenwart
The Contemporary Park of the Present

Einen Park zu gestalten, bedeutet Raum in Wert zu setzen. Das ist die eigentliche Idee des Parks. Ein definierter, an Grenzen und Inhalten ablesbarer Raum wird anfangs gegenüber der Wildnis, später gegenüber landwirtschaftlichen und industriellen, städtischen Nutzungs- und Funktionsräumen abgegrenzt, um das besondere Erlebnis zu zelebrieren. Park ist immer ein kultureller Kontrast zur Produktion der jeweiligen Zeit.

Welche Bedeutung hat dieses Park-Erlebnis heute? Der Park der Gegenwart ist eine starke Erzählung. Er erzählt von Natur, ihrem Versprechen und von der Befreiung aus ihr. Vor allem aber ist der Park das Narrativ von der Kultur der Begegnung, ihrer Zivilisierung. Nicht einfach ein Aufeinandertreffen, sondern ein kultiviertes Be(ob)achten, ein Interagieren, eine ungezwungene kollektive Individualität ist das Versprechen jedes gut besuchten Parks.

Zum ersten Mal in der Menschheitsgeschichte leben in der Gegenwart mehr Menschen in Städten als auf dem Land. In der Stadt gibt es keine Alternative mehr, kein Gegenüber zur urbanen Lebensform – außer im Park. Die Attraktivität des Urbanen verbindet sich mit Begriffen wie Lebensqualität, kulturelle sowie individuelle Freiheit und Vielfalt, der Verbindung von Wohnen und Arbeiten, Familie und Beruf, Sport und Gesundheit. Die Schattenseiten sind soziale Vereinzelung und Isolation, Luftverschmutzung, hoher Energieverbrauch, zunehmende Verdichtung und der Verlust von Frei- und Grünflächen.

Den Städten und Gemeinden – und hier insbesondere ihren Parks – kommt bei der Lösung sozialer, ökonomischer und ökologischer Herausforderungen eine bedeutende Rolle zu. Der Park ist erhabener Ausdruck des öffentlichen Raums als Verhandlungs- und Gestaltungsraum.

Der Park definiert die Räume, für die aus der Gesellschaft heraus eine besondere Verantwortung übernommen wird und die aus dem Alltag herausstechen. Stolz und

Designing a park means making effective use of space. That is the real idea behind a park. A defined space with recognisable borders and contents is sectioned off (initially from the wilderness and later from rural and industrial urban utilities and functional spaces) to celebrate a special experience. A park is always a cultural contrast to the productions of its period.

What significance does this park experience hold today? The contemporary park of the present is a strong narrative, telling of nature, of nature's promises, but also of the release from nature. Above all, however, the park is the narrative of the culture of encounter, of the civilising process. Not simply a coming together, but a cultivated process of observation and respect, an interaction, an informal collective individualism. That is the promise every well-attended park holds.

For the first time in history, more people are currently living in cities than in the countryside. In the city, there are no longer any alternatives, no counterpart to urban living forms – except in the park. The appeal of the urban sphere is associated with quality of life, cultural as well as individual freedom and diversity, the connection between living and working, family and profession, sport and health. The downsides are: social separation and isolation, air pollution, high consumption of energy, increasing density, and the loss of open and green areas.

Cities and communities play a significant role in tackling social, economic and ecological challenges – with much of this achieved by their parks. The park is a lofty expression of the public area as a negotiating space and an arena for creativity.

The park defines a space for which society takes on a special responsibility, standing out from everyday life. Pride and identity express themselves in the

Identität drücken sich im Park aus, weshalb anfangs Adelshäuser diese Form der Repräsentation wählten. Der Park war Ausdruck von Einfluss und Macht – auch über die Natur.

Das Bürgertum bediente sich mit wachsendem Einfluss – und wachsenden finanziellen Möglichkeiten – bald ähnlicher Mittel der Gestaltung von Raum als Park. Vom Garten als kleinteiligem Nutz- und Repräsentationsraum setzte sich der Park bald ab. Wer einen Park gestaltete, war sich seiner öffentlichen Verantwortung bewusst und wollte nicht nur im Privaten ordnend wirken.

Der Park ist seit jeher Ausdruck der Optimierung. Dabei wird die Entwicklung des Menschen aus der Natur heraus zur Grundlage (s)einer neuen Verantwortung gegenüber dieser. Im landschaftlichen wie im geometrischen Garten und Park können Freiheit, Individualität und Überraschung ihren Ausdruck finden. Horst Bredekamp erklärt dies anhand der Arbeiten des Philosophen Gottfried Wilhelm Leibniz, der wesentliche Anregungen zur Anlage des berühmten Barockgartens von Hannover-Herrenhausen gab. Leibniz bezog seine Vorstellungen von Natur und Kunst, seine Monadologie, auch auf die Gartengestaltung. Da kein Blatt dem anderen gleicht, erkannte er in der scheinbar unendlichen Formenvielfalt des barocken Parks die zutiefst individuelle Gestalt der Natur – und damit die Freiheit des Individuellen schlechthin.

So wird der Park im Barock und erst recht mit dem englischen Landschaftspark zum Laboratorium des Erkenntnisgewinns. Der Mensch, der sich darin bewegt, erfährt über die sinnliche Wahrnehmung neue Denkanstöße.

Die ökonomische Sinnhaftigkeit eines Parks, die heute aufwendig als Wert des öffentlichen Grüns berechnet werden kann, stand allerdings seit jeher in Zweifel. Parks zu gestalten ist immer auch Ausdruck von Überfluss, und wenn es der Überfluss an Ideen ist, um einem Mangel zu begegnen, wie es beispielsweise im Dessau-Wörlitzer Gartenreich der Fall war, dem Inbegriff unserer Parkkultur hier in Mitteleuropa seit über 200 Jahren.

Für einen Park konnte man sich auch verschulden, wie es insbesondere Fürst Pückler immer wieder bewies. Die kulturelle Botschaft, die Teilhabe an einer kultivierten Zukunft, siegte oftmals über pekuniäre Argumente.

Heute wissen wir, welche gesellschaftliche Bedeutung unsere Parks haben, als öffentlicher Raum der Städte und Landschaften und ebenso als Ausdruck der kommunalen und regionalen Identität.

Längst sind Städte und Gemeinden in die Rolle des Adels oder des Bürgertums hineingewachsen. Sie schöpfen Identität und bürgerschaftliche Zufriedenheit aus ihren

park, which is the reason why the aristocratic houses used parks to display their status. The park was an expression of influence and power – including power over nature.

As their influence grew – and their financial means increased – the bourgeoisie soon started designing spaces to create parks. The park soon became distinct from the garden as a small area for use and display. Whoever designed a park was aware of his/her public responsibility, and did not merely wish to impose order on their own private sphere.

The park has always been an expression of optimisation. Human development from nature becomes the basis of humanity's new responsibility towards nature. Freedom, individuality, and surprise find expression in rural as well as in geometric gardens and parks. Horst Bredekamp explains this by linking it to the work of the philosopher Gottfried Wilhelm Leibniz, who provided vital inspiration for creating the famous baroque gardens of the Hanover stately homes. Leibniz acquired his ideas from nature and art: his monadology, which he also applied to garden design. Since no two leaves are the same, he recognised in the apparent endless diversity of forms in the baroque park the deeply individual form of nature – and with this the freedom of the individual per se.

Thus the baroque tradition makes the park the laboratory of knowledge acquisition, with this being taken a step further by the English landscape garden. The person moving within this sphere discovers new thought-provoking impulses through sensory perception.

The economic significance of a park (which can be laboriously calculated today in terms of the value of public greenery) has always been in doubt. Designing parks is always an expression of abundance, even if this is an abundance of ideas to address shortages. As was the case, e.g., in the Dessau-Wörlitz Garden Realm, the epitome of our park culture here in Central Europe for over two hundred years.

It was also possible to get into debt for the sake of a park, as has been proven time and again, in particular by Count Pückler. The cultural message, the participation in a cultivated future, often prevailed over pecuniary arguments.

Today, we know the social significance of our parks, as public spaces for cities and landscapes and likewise as an expression of municipal and regional identity.

Parks. Und so mancher Park-Ermöglicher in der Politik und Verwaltung hat diesen Erfolg auch für die eigene Fortentwicklung nutzen können.

So ist heute der Entwurf eines Parks immer demokratisches Gemeingut. Die Repräsentation der Macht und dann die paternalistische Verantwortung wurden abgelöst vom Gemeinwesen-Charakter des Parks. Jeder Park ist ein repräsentatives Politikum, seine Gestaltung Gegenstand eines gesellschaftlichen Verhandlungsprozesses.

Zugleich ist seit der ebenfalls im Sinne einer politischen Stellungnahme zu lesenden Volksparkbewegung ebendiese Bewegung ein Schlüssel zur Idee des Parks.

Ungezwungenes, teils unkontrolliertes Sich-Bewegen führt uns heute in die Parks, ebenso wie die Begegnung und der ästhetische Genuss, die Teilhabe an einem repräsentativen und identitätsstiftenden Status der kommunalen, regionalen, demokratisch verfassten Gesellschaft.

Im Park treffen wir aufeinander. Im Park tragen wir miteinander Konflikte aus, die nicht durch soziale, berufliche, kulturelle oder ethische Strukturvorgaben vorgeprägt sind.

Die Neurourbanistik ist heute sogar in der Lage, den sozialpsychologischen Wert dieser Art der ungezwungenen Begegnung zu verstehen und zu bewerten. Städte können sich negativ auf die psychische Gesundheit auswirken – der Schlüssel zu einer wirksamen Gesundheitsstrategie in Metropolen liegt im öffentlichen Raum. „Wir brauchen vor allem Räume, die soziale Isolation verhindern und Teilhabe ermöglichen. Denn Begegnung, gegenseitiges Wahrnehmen, ist – gerade in sozial differenzierten Stadtgesellschaften – eine Schlüsselstrategie des gesellschaftlichen Zusammenhalts." (Mazda Adli) Konkret empfiehlt der Stressforscher eine „möglichst flexible Nutzung von öffentlichen Räumen"; je funktionsspezifischer ein Ort, desto mehr sei er für Stresserfahrungen seiner Nutzer verantwortlich.

Wie wollen wir uns und andere erleben, wie wollen wir gesehen werden? Bürgerinnen und Bürger, die im Park flanieren, joggen, trainieren, sich erholen, sich begegnen, stellen sich offen oder indirekt dieser Frage. „In den Park gehen" heißt nichts anderes, als sich der Öffentlichkeit zu stellen.

Nichts anderes streben auch Städte und Gemeinden an, die einen Park, seine Neu- oder Umgestaltung in Angriff nehmen. Sie wollen gesehen werden, sie wollen in ihre Parks einladen, Gäste sowie Bürgerinnen und Bürger gleichermaßen. Parks sind der Stolz der Städte und Gemeinden.

Angesichts der stark wachsenden Freizeit-Konkurrenz im digitalen und Medienzeitalter gilt dies ungebrochen. Wer sich virtuell mit anderen im Erlebnis trifft, will dies auch real tun, in der Kohlenstoffwelt unserer Parks. Parks werden

Cities and municipalities have long since taken on the role of the nobility or bourgeoisie. They derive identity and civic satisfaction from their parks. Some park enablers in politics and administration have also been able to use this success for their own advancement.

In this respect, designing a park today is always a democratic common property. Displaying power and thus paternalistic responsibility is replaced by a park with a communal character. Each park constitutes a prestigious political issue, and its design is the object of a civic negotiation process.

At the same time, it is this very movement that is the key to the park idea as it exists in the era of the people's park movement. It must also be understood in terms of a political statement.

Today, motivating factors to go to the park include casual, partly uncontrolled exercising, as well as meeting up and aesthetic pleasure, plus participation in a prestigious and identity-fostering element of municipal, regional, and democratically composed society.

We meet each other in the park, have conflicts that are not pre-shaped by social, professional, cultural or ethical structural requirements.

Neuro-urbanism today can even understand and evaluate the social-psychological value of this type of informal meeting. Cities can have a negative effect on mental health – the key to an effective health strategy in metropolitan cities lies in the public space. "Above all we need space to prevent social isolation and enable participation. Since meeting, mutually perceiving is – particularly in socially differentiated urban societies – a key strategy of social solidarity." (Mazda Adli) In concrete terms, the stress researcher recommends "as far as possible, flexible use of public space". The more function-specific a place is, the more it is responsible for the stress experiences of its users.

How do we want to experience ourselves and others and be seen? Civilians strolling, jogging, exercising, relaxing, meeting in the park ask themselves this openly or indirectly. "Being in the park" means nothing other than facing the public.

The cities and municipalities wanting to create a new park or park design or conversion also strive for the same thing. They want to be seen, to invite people to their parks, guests and inhabitants alike. Parks are a matter of pride for cities and municipalities.

In the light of the ever-increasing competition for our leisure time in the digital and media age, this

durch das gemeinsame Erleben zur kollektiven Erzählung der Menschen. Ob im Winter auf dem Schlitten oder auf dem Eis des Teiches, ob im Frühling angesichts der ersten Blüten, ob im Sommer, in der Kühle der „Frischluftschneise" Park in der Sonne liegend, oder im Herbst, beim Kastaniensammeln das trübe Licht aufsuchend – Park ist immer Entspannung und Erlebnis, Kommunikation und reale, dreidimensionale, multisensorische Erfahrung.

Der Park adelt, alle Akteure gewinnen mit dem Besuch eines Parks. Alle Akteure gewinnen auch mit dem Bau, der Pflege und der Gestaltung eines Parks. Das ist das Wichtigste. Alles andere ist Methode, Handwerk, Gestaltungskunst und Fantasie, ist Inspiration – die die Landschaftsarchitektur aus dem Ort nimmt. *Wie* geskes.hack dieses tun, wie sie einen Park entwerfen, mit wem zusammen, mit welchen Ideen und Instrumenten, ist Gegenstand dieses Buches.

Ein Buch zum Park der Gegenwart, zur Bedeutung des Gebauten als Überhöhung der menschengemachten Landschaft. Die kulturelle Überhöhung = Kontrast zur Natur wird abgelöst durch die Konstruktion der Natur, durch das Natursurrogat in der großmaßstäblichen wie in der städtischen Landschaft.

Gezeigt und in ihrer Idee vermittelt werden „grüne" Infrastrukturen in ihrem Verhältnis zur Landschaft, im Verhältnis zu einer im Park kultivierten Landschaft. Die meist hervorgeht aus einer Veränderung, einer Krise, einer Konversion. Der Park als Ausdruck der Transformation ist also das Thema. Das Buch stellt den Park anhand vielfältiger Beispiele ins Verhältnis zur Transformationsgesellschaft.

Die Gegenwart dauert drei Sekunden, sagen die Hirnforscher. Zwischen Reiz und Wahrnehmung und deren Verarbeitung erstreckt sich eine kurze, aber messbare Phase, in der wir in der Gegenwart leben. *Eben* und *vorhin* sind Vergangenheit und vollendete Vergangenheit, *gleich* und *später* sind die Zukunft.

Das Gegenwartsparadox (mit seinen vermeintlichen Zwängen, Unabdingbarkeiten) ist für die Gestaltung von Raum konstitutiv. Denn Raum, Landschaft allzumal, ist eine Geschichte, die sich im Kopf abspielt, ist eine Erzählung, die für eine kurze Phase sichtbar, denkbar wird. Man kann mit dieser „Geschichte" Bilder und damit Zukunft öffnen oder auch verschließen. Das macht die Frage nach der Bedeutung des Parks für unsere der Gegenwart verpflichtete Transformationskultur so spannend.

Genau diese kurze Phase der Wahrnehmung ist Gegenstand der Landschaftsarchitektur. Die Komposition von Raum ist dieser Wahrnehmung verpflichtet, hat ihr Angebote zu machen. Denn Raum, Landschaft im Besonderen, ist

continues to apply. Anyone meeting up virtually with others will also want to do this in the real world, in the carbon world of our parks. Through joint experiences, parks become people's collective narratives. Whether tobogganing and skating on the ice in winter, looking at the first blossoms in spring, lying in the sun enjoying the coolness of a "fresh air lane" park in summer, or collecting chestnuts in the fading light of autumn – a park always involves relaxation and living, communication, and a real, three-dimensional, multi-sensory experience.

A park enobles; everyone gains from visiting a park. People also gain from the construction, maintenance, and design of a park. Everything else is method, handicraft, design art, fantasy, inspiration: the taking of the landscape architecture from the location. *How* geskes.hack do this, how they design a park, with whom and with which ideas and tools, is the subject matter of this book.

It is a book about the contemporary park of the present, about the significance of what is built as an elevation of the man-made landscape. The notion of cultural elevation = contrast to nature is replaced by the construction of nature, by nature surrogacy on a large scale, as in the urban landscape.

"Green" infrastructure elements and their relationship to the landscape are displayed in this book, and the ideas behind them are explained. This takes place in relation to a landscape cultivated in the park. Usually, this landscape stems from a change, a crisis, a conversion. Thus, our theme is the park as an expression of transformation. The book relates the park to the transformative society, based on a diverse range of examples.

The present lasts three seconds, according to brain researchers. Between stimulus and perception and the processing thereof lies a short but measurable phase in which we live in the present. *Just now* and *before* are the past and past perfect, *shortly* and *later* are the future.

The paradox of the present (with its supposed constraints and imperative nature) is constitutive for the design of space. As space – landscape, certainly – is a story that plays out in our minds. It is a narrative that becomes visible and conceivable for a short period. With this "story" we can open up images – and thus the future. Or we may also close the images and the future down. This is what makes the significance of the park

assoziativ, nicht absolut. Die Schönheit liegt im Auge des Betrachters, sie bedingt und ermöglicht das ästhetische Urteil.

Aktuelle Raumbegriffe, also Vermessung, Herrschaft, Ordnung einerseits und Freiheit andererseits, sind zugleich Versprechen, Identifikationen. Wie binden Landschaftsarchitekten diese Raumbegriffe, ihre konkreten Ausdrücke, ein in eine Erzählung, in das Narrativ einer Stadt, einer Landschaft, einer Region?

Wir sind dieser Art des Lesens des Raumes verpflichtet. Die Landschaftsarchitektur erzählt dabei nichts Vergangenes, nichts Zukünftiges, sondern assoziiert Gegenwarten. Landschaftsarchitektur ist keine Museologie, keine Forschung, kein Szenario, sondern äußerst real für alle Sinne. Und vermittelt auf diese Weise, durch das Park-Narrativ, Bezüge zur Vergangenheit und Zukunft als gegenwärtige Impressionen.

Das In-den-Park-Gehen ist konstitutiv für die Park-Idee der Gegenwart. Park ist dort, wo sich Menschen im Erlebnis treffen.

Der Park ist Wahrnehmungsraum, ein Raum für drei Sekunden. Der Park als ein solcher Erlebensraum für Erinnerungen, für Visionen, für Hoffnungen entsteht aus der Intensität des Gegenwartserlebens. Und dieses Gegenwartserleben dosieren geskes.hack in ihren Entwürfen – und damit in den gebauten Parks.

Thies Schröder

so exciting for our culture of transformation, so committed to the present.

This short phase of perception is the subject matter of landscape architecture. The composition of space is committed to this perception, and has to appeal to it. After all, space – and landscape in particular – is associative, not absolute. The beauty lies in the eye of the beholder, and aesthetic judgement is contingent upon it, and enabled by it.

Current spatial concepts, i.e. surveying, governance, arrangement on the one hand and freedom on the other, are also promises and factors of identity. How do landscape architects integrate these spatial concepts and their concrete expressions to form a single narrative of a city, a landscape, a region?

We are dedicated to this way of reading spaces. This means the landscape architecture says nothing about the past, nothing about the future. Instead, it unites the different "presents". Landscape architecture is not museology, not research, not a scenario. It is extremely real in every sense. In this way, through the narrative of the park, it conveys references to the past and future as present impressions.

Being in the Park is constitutive for the park idea of the present. The park is the place where people meet to experience.

The park is a space of perception for that "three seconds". The park as such is a space of experience for memories, visions, hopes arising from the intensity of experiencing the present. geskes.hack distil this in their designs – and thus also in the implemented parks.

Thies Schröder

Waldbühne, Reichenbach

Forest Stage, Reichenbach

BESTAND
EXISTING STRUCTURES

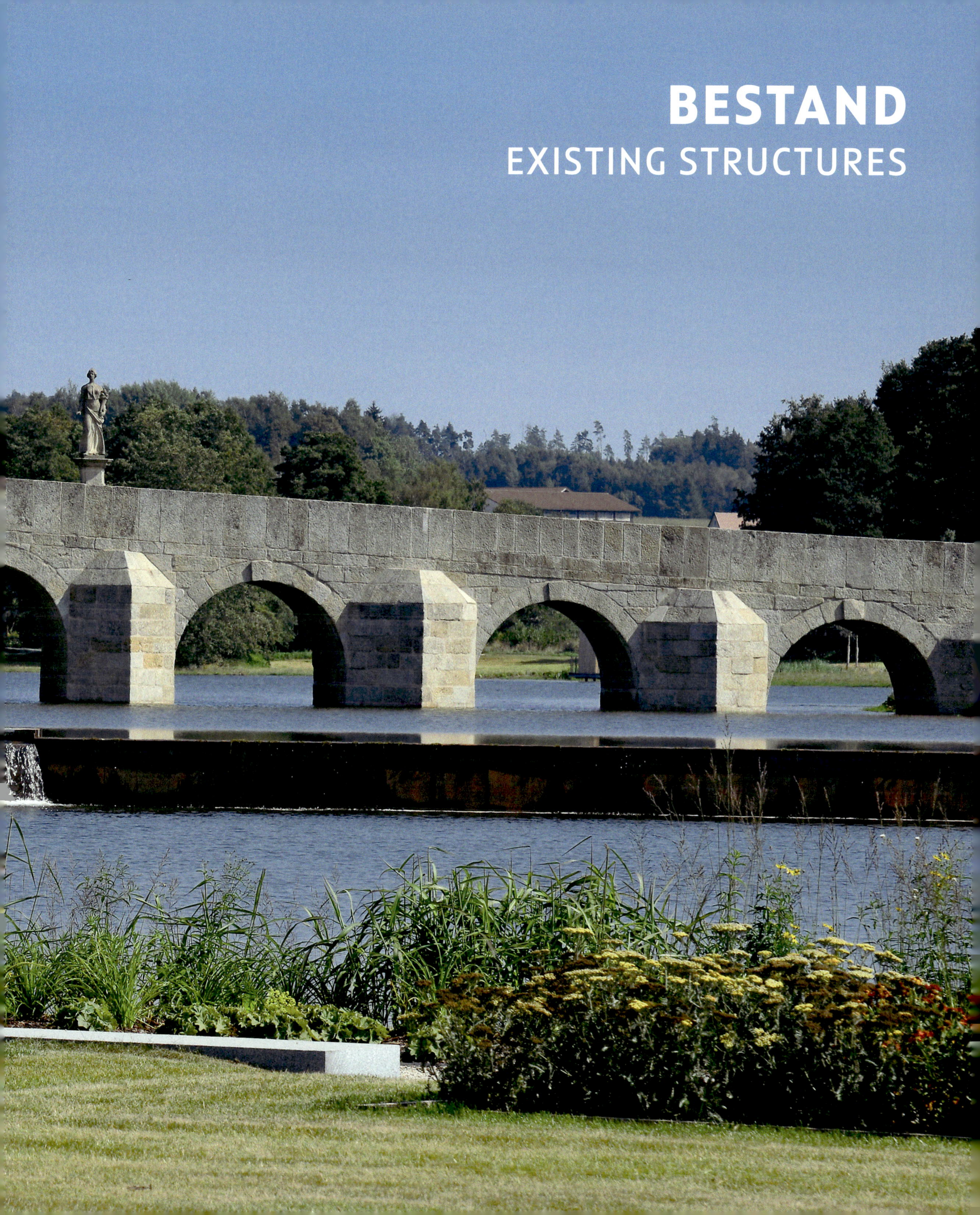

MASSSTÄBLICHKEIT
PROPORTION

ÜBERRASCHUNG
SURPRISE

AKTIVITÄT UND WOHLGEFÜHL
ACTIVITY AND WELL-BEING

SPIEL ALS STEIGERUNG
PLAY AS ENHANCEMENT

ERZÄHLUNGEN IM PARK

TALES IN THE PARK

In den Park gehen
Being in the Park

Im Gespräch mit Kristina Hack und Christof Geskes
Talking to Kristina Hack and Christof Geskes

Welche Bedeutung hat der Park für geskes.hack?
CG: Der Arbeitsschwerpunkt unseres Büros liegt auf diesem Thema Park. Natürlich haben wir auch andere Aufgaben, wie die Gestaltung von Plätzen oder Promenaden, aber unser Schwerpunkt sind diese großen Parks. Es ist unsere Kompetenz, Qualitäten in größeren Strukturen zu entwickeln.

Gibt es Haltungen oder Regeln, Fähigkeiten und Begabungen des Büros geskes.hack, die sich durch die Entwürfe für die unterschiedlichsten Parks hindurch zeigen?
CG: Wichtig ist die übergeordnete städtebauliche Einbindung. Also die Frage, wie sich ein Park verhält zu seiner umgebenden Stadt. Daraus generieren wir Parkeingänge, Übergänge, Zwischenräume, Sichtbezüge oder thematische Gärten. Es geht uns jeweils um die enge Verzahnung von Stadt und Park, also darum, dass nicht beide jeweils autistisch nebeneinanderliegen, sondern sich stark aufeinander beziehen.
KH: Wir analysieren und respektieren den Bestand. Dazu gehören vorhandene Vegetationsstrukturen ebenso wie vorhandene Wege, Nutzungsspuren. Wir stülpen einem Ort nicht einfach ein bei uns im Kopf entstandenes Konzept über, sondern gehen aus von Bestehendem. Wir betrachten sehr intensiv, wie sich Stadt in ihrem Park darstellt, welche Identität der Stadtbürgerschaft in einem Park zum Ausdruck kommt und zum Ausdruck kommen soll. Und wir untersuchen, wo der Bestand Qualitäten bietet oder Eingriffe zur Optimierung braucht. Oder wo der Bestand so katastrophal ist, dass er komplett beseitigt werden muss.
Das machen wir auch in Wettbewerben so, und zwar in Teams, in denen wir uns intensiv mit unserer Wahrnehmung des Bestandes auseinandersetzen. Die Ergebnisse, die sich

What is the significance of parks for geskes.hack?
CG: Our work is focused on the park theme. Of course, we have other tasks, such as designing squares or promenades, but our focus is on these large parks. Our expertise is developing the right qualities in larger structures.

Are there attitudes or rules, skills and talents in the geskes.hack office demonstrated throughout the designs for the widely varying parks?
CG: What is important is the primary urban integration. This is the question of how a park relates to its surrounding city. From this, we generate entrances to the park, crossovers, spaces, visual references or themed gardens. What is important to us is the interlinking of city and park, meaning that they are not just incompatibly located next to each other but strongly relate to each other.
KH: We analyse and respect the existing structures, including vegetation structures as well as existing paths, traces of use. We don't simply impose a concept we have developed in our minds on a place; instead, we start with what already exists. We take a close look at how the city presents itself in its park, what kind of identity a park expresses or should express for its citizens. And we examine where the existing structures offer good qualities or need interventions to optimise. Or where the existing structure is so disastrous that it needs to be removed completely.
We also take the same approach to competitions; working in teams, we engage intensely with our perception of the existing structures. The results emerging

daraus entwickeln, sind für den Entwurf von zentraler Bedeutung. Teils gehen sie über Anforderungen, die in einer Auslobung oder einer Aufgabenbeschreibung eines Wettbewerbs formuliert werden, hinaus.
Als Beispiel möchte ich einen Wettbewerb nennen, in dem die Auslobung den Erhalt einer Sporthalle verpflichtend vorsah, die an einer wichtigen Schnittstelle zwischen Stadt und Park platziert war. Wir Landschaftsarchitekten planen aber nicht für die nächsten zehn oder fünfzehn Jahre, sondern für die nächsten fünfzig oder hundert Jahre. Und an diesem Ort einer zentralen städtebaulichen Verbindung störte die Sporthalle. Da mussten wir uns als Landschaftsarchitekten herausnehmen zu sagen, dass diese Halle dort weg muss, um die Parklandschaft zu komplettieren. Das wurde dann eine zentrale Aussage unseres Entwurfs.

Holztreppe, Kienbergpark Berlin

Wooden Stairway, Kienbergpark Berlin

BESTAND

Ein weiteres Beispiel für diese Genauigkeit ist der Kienbergsteig, eines der unauffälligeren Elemente im Kienbergpark in Berlin-Marzahn. Viele Besucher der IGA 2017 haben den Kienbergsteig, diese Holztreppe, gar nicht bewusst entdeckt. Doch diese unspektakuläre Geste ist uns wichtig, weil sie ein Schlüssel ist für das Gefüge des Parks. Man geht den Berg auf diesem Steig ein Stück hinab und kommt so auf ein Plateau mit einem großartigen Blick über das Wuhletal und auf die Großsiedlung Marzahn-Hellersdorf. Diesen kleinen Abstieg zum Plateau gab es rudimentär im Bestand, eine Art Trampelpfad oder Spur im Gelände. Wir haben ihn aus der schon erprobten Aneignung, also aus dem Bestand heraus, weiterentwickelt. Wir haben diese eher unauffällige Situation des Ankommens auf diesem Plateau gestaltet. Dieses Ankommen, diese kleine Geste, ist uns ebenso wichtig wie das Plateau selbst. Denn in einem Park ist die Verbindung und nicht allein die Platzierung von Höhepunkten bedeutsam.
So entsteht das Wohlfühlen insbesondere aus unserer Genauigkeit im Ansehen des Bestandes – und zwar mit vielen Augen. Die passende Maßstäblichkeit wird später von den Besuchern empfunden, nicht analysiert. Und um den Besuchern diese passende Maßstäblichkeit zu gewähren, kommt es auf vermeintlich Nebensächliches besonders an.

from this are of central importance for the design. In part, they go beyond the requirements laid down in a tender or a competition task description.
One example, a competition in which the preservation of a sports hall was stated as compulsory in the tender; the hall was situated at an important interface between the city and the park. However, we as landscape architects don't plan for the next ten or fifteen years but for the next fifty or hundred years. And in this case the sports hall was in the way because it was located at a central urban connection. As landscape architects we had to step back and say, this hall has to go to complete the park landscape. This then became a central statement of our design.

EXISTING STRUCTURES

Another example of this accuracy is Kienbergsteig, one of the more inconspicuous elements in Kienberg Park in Berlin-Marzahn. Many visitors to the International Garden Exhibition 2017 weren't even consciously aware of this Kienbergsteig, this wooden stairway. Yet this non-spectacular feature is important to us because it is key to the park's fabric. You use the stairway to go a short way down the hill, arriving at a plateau offering a fantastic view over the Wuhle valley and the large Marzahn-Hellersdorf housing estate. This short descent to the plateau existed in a rudimentary form, a kind of trampled path or track in the terrain. We

Kienbergterrassen, Berlin
Kienberg Terraces, Berlin

MASSSTÄBLICHKEIT

Wie bringt diese Augenhöhe die landschaftsarchitektonische Arbeit voran?

KH: Immer wieder stellen wir fest, und zwar besonders in kleineren Städten, wie stark die Bewohner, Gemeinderäte, Bürgermeister oder Bauamtsleiter mit ihrem Ort verbunden sind. Das motiviert uns, und wir treten mit diesen Bürgern und ihren Vertretern in Kontakt und in eine Diskussion.

Doch auf Augenhöhe arbeiten heißt nicht, dass keine großen Gesten entstehen. Ein Beispiel: die große Achse, die in Hemer auf den Berg führt. Sie haben eine solche Geste in dieser Dimension selten gesehen. Dennoch ist genau diese Geste in dieser Dimension im Rahmen einer gemeinsamen Diskussion entstanden.

Wir suchen also *vor Ort* die Gesten, die an den jeweiligen Ort, auch an das jeweilige Budget, angepasst sind. Wenn uns die Nutzer dann bestätigen, dass wir den richtigen Maßstab gefunden haben, dann ist genau das offenbar unser Können.

Ist dieses „Genau-Treffen" abhängig von der Art der Kommunikation?

CG: Die Ästhetik, die wir entwickeln in der Landschaftsarchitektur, muss natürlich ins Umfeld passen, wir können ja nicht irgendetwas aufsetzen auf den Ort. In einen kleinen Ort mit mittelalterlicher Prägung passt nach unserem gestalterischen Empfinden kein Entwurf, der von der Pop-Art inspiriert ist.

KH: Dabei ist unsere Haltung nicht zu verwechseln mit einer Rekonstruktion des Vorgefundenen oder Vergangenen. Wir wollen bei jedem Projekt ganz bewusst einen modernen Aspekt neu hinzufügen, und das nicht laut und auf Effekte bedacht.

Das kann gelingen durch die Materialität, durch den Stein, durch die Farbigkeit, durch die Vegetation, durch die passende Größe von Objekten und Elementen, durch die Ausrichtung, durch Blickbezüge.

CG: Ein anderer gestalterischer Aspekt, der mir besonders am Herzen liegt, ist der, dass wir vor Ort versuchen, besondere topografische Lagen aufzuspüren. Das Thema Topografie und Terrasse ist für uns ein ganz zentrales. Eigentlich versuchen wir immer, bemerkenswerte Geländeformen zu einem aufregenden neuen Element der Landschaft weiterzuentwickeln, indem wir sie, beispielsweise als Terrasse, als besonderen Ort inszenieren ...

KH: ... also auch überhöhen, freistellen, abräumen, was stört.

refined it from appropriated tried-and-tested elements, i.e. from the existing structures. Therefore we designed this rather inconspicuous arrangement for arriving on this plateau. This small gesture is just as important to us as the plateau itself. After all, in a park the connections are significant, not merely the placing of highlights.

This is how a feeling of well-being arises, with emphasis on our precision in handling existing structures – with many eyes on the problem. The apt sense of proportion will be felt, not analysed, by the visitors. Granting the visitors this apt sense of proportion is, more than anything else, about the supposed insignificant factors.

PROPORTION

How does this working on an equal footing promote the landscape work?

KH: We have repeatedly determined, particularly in the case of smaller cities, how connected residents, municipal councils, mayors or heads of building authorities are with their town. This motivates us and we communicate with these citizens and their representatives.

Yet working on an equal footing does not mean that no bigger gestures emerge. One example of this is the large axis line that leads to the hill in Hemer. This type of gesture in this dimension is rare. Nevertheless, it is precisely this gesture in this dimension that emerged in the course of a joint discussion.

We therefore look for the gestures *on site* that are adapted to the specific location and also to the specific budget. If the users confirm we have found the right scale, then this is obviously our talent.

Is this "accuracy" dependent on the type of communication?

CG: The landscape architecture we develop naturally has to fit into the surroundings. We can't place just anything in the town. A design inspired by pop-art based on our creative skills would not fit into a small town with a medieval character.

KH: At the same time, our attitude shouldn't be mistaken for the reconstructing of existing or past structures. In every project, we aim to consciously add a new modern aspect, but not in a loud way and not for effect.

This is achieved through the materials, through stone, colour, vegetation, adroit sizing of objects and

Himmelstreppe, Hemer

Stairway to Heaven, Hemer

elements, through the orientation, perspectives.

CG: Another design aspect that is particularly close to my heart is endeavouring to trace special topographic locations on site. The topic of topography and terrace is a very central one for us. In fact, we always attempt to further refine remarkable terrains into exciting new elements of the landscape by presenting them as special places. As a terrace, for example ...

KH: ... This also means super-elevating, cropping, clearing away distracting elements.

Forumsplatz mit Himmelsspiegel, Hemer

Forum Square with Sky Mirror, Hemer

Was würde passieren, wenn geskes.hack den Auftrag bekämen, auf einem komplett weißen Papier, ohne jegliche Orientierung an Bestehendem, einen Park zu entwerfen?

KH: Das ist genau das, worauf ich schon in der Lehre an der Universität immer wieder hingewiesen habe. Entwerfen auf einem weißen Blatt – das geht nicht. Selbst wenn ich einen Dachgarten gestalte, der ja kaum Bezug zum Umfeld hat, der quasi frei schwebt, beziehe ich mich in diesem Entwurf auf das Gebäude, auf den Ort des Betretens, auf den Ausblick. Und auch wenn ich einen Garten plane, der ja von der Umgebung eher geschützt und abgegrenzt ist, beziehe ich mich auf die Landschaft, auf den Ort, das Klima.

Es kommt zum Schluss, bei aller intensiven Analyse des Bestandes, der Kommunikation mit den Nutzern, den Methoden und Definitionen von Materialität, immer ein Park heraus, ein Park von geskes.hack. Obwohl es nicht den einen Stil von geskes.hack gibt, die eine Entwurfshaltung, gibt Ihr Büro dem Ort immer etwas dazu, was ein Park ist, ein typischer Park. Was sind Ihre Erwartungen an den Park, was macht Ihnen an einem Park besonderen Spaß?

KH: Genau das. Wenn wir mitbekommen, dass die Leute auf unseren Park reagieren. Wenn ich ganz ohne Rolle und Aufgabe durch den Kienbergpark in Marzahn laufe und sehe, dass die Bürger sich dort aufhalten, dass sich ein stimmiges Bild ergibt, ein lebendiges Bild, dass der Park angenommen wird, wenn durch die Gestaltung ein Wandel geschieht und die Schönheit eines Ortes – auch in schwierigem städtebaulichen Umfeld – neu oder wieder ins Bewusstsein

What would happen if geskes.hack were awarded the commission to design a park on a completely blank sheet of paper without any orientation on existing structures?

KH: This is exactly what I have previously repeatedly pointed out when teaching at the university. Designing on a blank piece of paper – it's not possible. Even designing a roof garden that has hardly any relation to the surroundings and thus is practically hovering freely, I reference the building in this design, the place of access, the view. And even if I am planning a garden that is protected and cut off from its surroundings, I reference the landscape, to the place, the climate.

At the end of all the intensive analyses of the existing structures, communication with users, applying methods and defining material qualities, the end result is always a park, a geskes.hack, park. Although there is one style and one attitude to design attributed to geskes.hack, this is a firm that always gives the location something more in addition to a park, a typical park. What are your expectations of the park and what aspect of a park do you particularly enjoy?

KH: It's precisely the part where we hear that people are reacting to our park. When I walk through the Kienberg Park in Marzahn with no role or task of any kind to perform and see that the residents are spending time there, that a coherent picture has been created, a scene with plenty of life, when a change has occurred thanks to the design and the people have become aware of the beauty of a place for the first time, or become aware of it once again – perhaps in a difficult urban environment – that's what makes me

kommt, dann freut mich das. Park wird, wenn er attraktiv ist, überall ähnlich genutzt, in der Großstadt wie auch im ländlichen Raum. Das zeigt, wie allgemein verständlich und kulturell prägend das Thema Park ist. Die Anonymität wird aufgebrochen im Park; der Park wird zum verbindenden Element, durch und in dem die Leute miteinander in Kommunikation treten – in einer ästhetischen Gesamtschau und -stimmung.

happy. If a park is attractive, it will be used in a similar way everywhere, in big cities as well as in rural areas. This shows how universally intelligible and how shaped by a shared culture the park theme is. In a park, anonymity breaks up; the park becomes a unifying element through and in which people communicate with each other – through the overall aesthetic look and mood.

ÜBERRASCHUNG

Also Anonymität aufbrechen, Begegnung als die zentrale Funktion des Parks?

CG: Ja, und dafür ist wichtig, dass man die Leute überrascht.

KH: Wenn die Leute plötzlich quasi überwältigt sind, durch eine betonte Weite oder die Intimität in den Wassergärten in Marzahn, dann hebt das die Stimmung – und die Bereitschaft zur Kommunikation.

CG: Dieses Überraschungsmoment in der Landschaftsarchitektur, das Entdecken, gelingt beispielsweise mit einem Quellgarten, der eine ganz besondere, auch physisch spürbare Atmosphäre bietet. Oder wir überraschen mit einem floral gestalteten Senkgarten in einer Flussaue, wie in Reichenbach. Oder mit der Römerbastion in Zülpich: Am Ende eines langweiligen landwirtschaftlichen Weges tut sich plötzlich eine Aussicht auf, eine gestaltete Landschaftsterrasse, mit Geschichtsbezug, aber vor allem mit der Lebendigkeit der Gegenwart.

KH: Uns erfreut auch, wenn die kräftigen Bilder, die wir im Kopf hatten, nach gewisser Zeit der Entwicklung aufgegangen sind, wenn durch Vegetation und Modellierung aus unseren Skizzen reale Räume entstehen.

CG: Und uns erfreut, wenn wir in den Parkanlagen, in denen wir uns immer sehr viel Mühe geben mit den Spielplätzen, erkennen, wie unterschiedliche Altersgruppen die Spielplätze annehmen. Auf dem großen Wasserspielplatz in Berlin-Marzahn beispielsweise sind Kinder und Jugendliche im Alter von einem bis achtzehn Jahren sowie Erwachsene aktiv – genau das war die Idee. Offenbar konnten wir den Nerv treffen und etwas anbieten, mit dem sich die Besucher gerne beschäftigen, wo sie sich betätigen, wo Freude aufkommt.

SURPRISE

So this means that breaking up anonymity and meeting up are the central function of the park?

CG: Yes, and one important aspect of this is surprising people.

KH: If people are suddenly overwhelmed by an emphasised vastness or intimacy in the water gardens in Marzahn, then this lifts their spirits – and makes them more willing to communicate.

CG: This element of surprise in landscape architecture, the discovery aspect, was successfully achieved, for instance, in a spring garden that offers a very special atmosphere that is also physically tangible. We have also surprised people with a florally designed sunken garden in a floodplain, at Reichenbach. Or the Roman bastion in Zülpich: at the end of a tedious landscape path, suddenly a view emerges, a designed landscape terrace with a link to history, but above all linked to the vigour of the present.

Quellgarten, Kienbergpark Berlin

Spring Garden, Kienbergpark Berlin

AKTIVITÄT UND WOHLGEFÜHL

KH: Die Kommunikation der Menschen *in* der Parkanlage ist uns wichtig, die Menschen werden aus ihrer Individualität herausgeholt in den Park, dort kommen sie miteinander in Kontakt.
CG: Der Fotograf Hanns Joosten hat für dieses Buch auch unsere älteren Anlagen erneut fotografiert – und diese Fotos zeigen uns, welches Leben in diesen Parks bis heute Raum findet. In Hemer gibt es täglich Veranstaltungen, der Park ist zum Zentrum des städtischen Lebens geworden. Ähnliches sehen wir in Reichenbach oder Tirschenreuth. In Zülpich ist der Park zu einem großen Freibad geworden, mit Paddlern, Surfern, Tretbooten. Es brummt wie verrückt. Der Pflegezustand überzeugt dennoch. Die Parks werden offenbar so geliebt, dass sie auch gepflegt werden.
KH: Es gelingt uns als Landschaftsarchitekten, in diesen Parks nicht zu viel zu machen, sie nicht gartenkünstlerisch zu überladen. Unsere Parks werden oft als entspannend empfunden, weil sie angemessen sind. Vieles wirkt nach kurzer Zeit einfach „normal" – und das ist dann gut.

Bleibt denn die Landschaftsarchitektur auch nach Jahren noch beeindruckend, vielleicht auch aufregend an manchen Orten? Was reizt, weiterhin und wiederholt in den Park zu gehen? Selbst im digitalen Informations- und Kommunikationszeitalter?
CG: Dieses In-den-Park-Gehen, also nicht durch den Park gehen, am Park entlanggehen, ist für unsere Arbeit das wichtigste Ziel. Wenn wir Gesten formulieren und Akzente setzen, sind diese deutlich und stark, aber eben nicht zu viele. Auch ohne aufwendige, pflegebedürftige Vegetation müssen unsere Parks nach dem ersten Jahr, häufig dem Jahr einer Gartenschau, funktionieren.
KH: Die eigentlichen Entwürfe, die ersten Ideen, bearbeitet bei uns ein kleines Team. Es gibt also unterschiedliche Einflüsse, aber eine ähnliche Haltung. Und diese Haltung des Büros basiert – neben der intensiven Ortskenntnis – genau auf dieser Frage: Wie würden wir, wenn wir vor Ort leben würden, das jeweilige Stück Landschaft oder Natur oder Gartenkunst zu schätzen wissen, was würde uns fehlen, was würde uns bereichern als Bürger? Was würde mir gefallen, wo möchte ich gern sitzen, wo möchte ich hinschauen? Was würde ich dort vor Ort als Rentner machen, als Mutter, als Kind? Wie würde ich diesen Raum nutzen wollen, zu Fuß, mit dem Rollator, auf dem Fahrrad? Wohin würde ich mich als Jugendlicher gerne zurückziehen, wo sichtbar werden?

Tagebausee, Zülpich

Mining Lake, Zülpich

KH: We are also pleased when the powerful images we had in our heads come to life after a certain period of development, when real spaces are produced from our sketches through vegetation and modelling.
CG: In the case of park areas where we have also made a great deal of effort with the playgrounds, it also pleases us when we see different age groups appreciating the playgrounds. For instance, children and young people aged from one to eighteen – and also adults – are active at the big water playground in Berlin-Marzahn. That was always the idea. We have obviously been able to strike a chord and offer something the visitors can enjoy and where they can have fun.

ACTIVITY AND WELL-BEING

KH: People communicating *in* the park is important to us. People reach out of their individuality in the park, get in contact with each other.
CG: The photographer Hanns Joosten has taken photos of our older sites for this book – and these photos show us the life that still exists in these park to the present day. Daily events are held in Hemer, and the park has become a centre of urban life. We can see similar scenes in Reichenbach or Tirschenreuth. In Zülpich, the park has become a large outdoor swimming pool, used by paddlers, surfers, pedal boaters. It's absolutely buzzing. Nevertheless, the standard of maintenance makes a convincing impression. The parks are obviously taken good care of because they are so popular.
kh: We are successful as landscape architects because we don't do too much, and we don't leave the parks artistically cluttered. Our parks are often perceived as relaxing because they are appropriate. After a short time, many things appear simply to be "normal" – and that is a good thing.

Does landscape architecture still remain impressive even after many years? In many cases, can it even stay exciting? What is the incentive to continue to go to the park? Even in the age of digital information and communication?
CG: This Being in the Park, i.e. not walking through the park, along the park, is the most important goal for our work. When we create gestures and emphasise features, we do it clearly and strongly, just not too often. Our parks have to continue to function after the

Kletter-Ei, Gießen

Climbing Egg, Gießen

first year (frequently the year of a garden exhibition) even without elaborate, high-maintenance vegetation.

KH: The actual designs, the initial ideas, are developed in a small team. Thus, there are various influences but a similar approach. Besides the deep knowledge of the location, this attitude of the office is based on precisely this question: how would we appreciate the specific piece of landscape or nature of the garden art if we lived there? What would we miss, what would enrich us as citizens? What would I like, where would I like to sit, in which direction would I like to look? What would I do in this park if I were a pensioner, a mother, a child? How would I want to use this space on foot, on a walking frame, on the bike? As a young person, where would I like to retreat to, where would I be visible?

The needs of the various groups within the population always impose obligations upon us. Not only must there be something there for everybody, but the design solution must have a joint benefit for all these groups.

Diese Bedürfnisse unterschiedlicher Gruppen der Bevölkerung sind für uns immer Verpflichtung, und es muss wirklich für jeden nicht nur etwas dabei sein, sondern die Entwurfslösung muss für alle diese Gruppen ein gemeinsamer Gewinn sein.

Ist das Hineinversetzen in dritte Personen eine Methode des Büros, zu Entwürfen zu kommen? Es erinnert an den Persona-Ansatz aus den Sozialwissenschaften, dem Marketing oder der Produktentwicklung.

KH: Ich spiele das in meinem Kopf so durch, denke in Varianten, generationenübergreifend, verbinde diese dann. Wenn die Methode so heißt, okay. Wir haben sie für unser Entwerfen entwickelt.

Was wir allerdings nicht tun, ist die Bürger zu fragen, welches Sitzmöbel sie denn gerne hätten. Da unterscheiden wir uns wohl von klassischer Marktforschung. Diese Art der Partizipation führt zu keinem Ergebnis. Dafür gibt es ja die in ihrer Gestaltungskomptenz ausgebildeten Landschaftsarchitekten, die dann entsprechend die Dinge verorten.

Is empathising with others the method of the office in creating designs? It calls to mind the "persona approach" as used in the social sciences, marketing, and product development.

KH: I go through it in my mind. I think of the variations, of cross-generationality. Then I combine all of these. If that is what the method is called, then that's okay. We developed it for our designs.

However, what we don't do is ask the citizens what type of seating they'd like. This is where we no doubt differ from classic market research. This type of participation yields no result. That is what landscape architects trained in design skills are there for, so that they can locate the relevant items.

Wollen oder sollen wir in den Park gehen?

CG: Ja, aber nicht im Sinne der Pädagogik. Wir bieten Ästhetik an.

KH: Da sind wir sehr bestimmt.

Do we want to or should we go to the park?

CG: Yes, but not for educational reasons. We offer aesthetics.

KH: We are very clear in this respect.

Also Geschmacksbildung durch ästhetisches Angebot? Wie in den Parks der Aufklärung?

This means developing taste by offering aesthetic qualities? Like in the educational parks?

KH: Der Kletterparcours beispielsweise muss nicht nur zum Klettern einladen, sondern auch zum Park passen, zu den anderen Elementen der Ausstattung. Die Parkanlage muss aus einem Guss sein, durch alle Maßstäbe und Elemente hindurch. Da muss die Farbigkeit passen, die Materialität.
CG: Allerdings nicht im Sinne von Uniformität, denn jeder Ort ist durch einen eigenen Charakter ausgewiesen. Weder das Individuelle allein ist für uns das Ziel noch das Einheitliche einer Parkanlage.

KH: The climbing route, for example, needs to invite people to climb, but it must also suit the park and the other elements of the fixtures. The park complex must be of a piece, throughout all benchmarks and elements. The colouring and materials must be appropriate.
CG: However, they should not be uniform, since each place is identified by its own character. Neither individuality nor uniformity is the goal for us in designing the park complex.

SPIEL ALS STEIGERUNG

Ist das In-den-Park-Gehen ein spielerisches Ziel?
CG: Ja, der Homo ludens ist eine unserer wesentlichen Annahmen. Das Spiel ermöglicht Begegnung, Kommunikation, Ins-Gespräch-Kommen. Wir alle kennen das von den Besuchen auf einem Spielplatz.
KH: Das ist genau das, was in der Zukunft, in unserem digitalen Zeitalter, stärker ausgebaut werden muss. Die Angebote im öffentlichen Raum müssen noch stärker, noch attraktiver werden, auch noch spielerischer.
Wenn einem Bürgermeister zum Beispiel zum Thema Attraktivität seiner Gemeinde für Jugendliche nur noch ein WLAN-Hotspot einfällt, werden wir neugierig. An diesen Punkt müssen wir ran – mit besseren Ideen, mit mehr Fantasie. Denn für die Entwicklung von Kindern und Jugendlichen haben wir als Landschaftsarchitekten eine besondere Verantwortung.

PLAY AS ENHANCEMENT

Is Being in the Park a playful goal?
CG: Yes. Homo ludens is one of our key assumptions. Play enables meeting, communication, beginning a conversation. We all know this from visiting a playground.
KH: This is exactly what must be developed even more in the future, in our digital age. What is on offer in public space needs to expand, to be made more attractive and even more playful.
For example, if all a mayor can come up with in terms of ideas for attractions in his or her community for young people is a WLAN hotspot, our curiosity is aroused. This is where we need to take action – with better ideas, more imagination. After all, we as landscape architects have a special responsibility for the development of children and young people.

Kann die Landschaftsarchitektur in Konkurrenz zur Erlebnisvielfalt und -intensität des Virtuellen mithalten?
CG: In den Park zu gehen, heißt eher Gegenwelten anzubieten. Im Park können Dinge stattfinden, die andernorts nicht stattfinden können. Ich habe mal Filmsequenzen neu zusammengeschnitten von Szenen, die in Parks spielen, von *Hair* über *Gorky Park* bis zu Paul Austers *Manhattan Stories*. Park ist da immer auch Raum, der zur normierten Welt im Kontrast steht. Park muss das Erleben von Gegenwelten zumindest zulassen, am besten anregen, von der Kontemplation bis zur Aktion.
So löst der Quellgarten in den Gärten der Welt eine ganz andere Herzfrequenz aus als der Aufstieg auf den Wolkenhain.

Spielplatz der Atolle, Schwerin

Playground of the Atolls, Schwerin

Spiel-Wal in den Gärten der Welt, Berlin

Play Whale in the Gardens of the World, Berlin

Oder die Vulkane in Schwerin mit ihren 7 Metern Höhe – für Kinder eine enorme Herausforderung.

KH: Besonderheiten in Farbe, Form und Größe gehören für uns zum guten Park dazu. Aber auch Retro-Angebote haben ihren Reiz und stiften Vergnügen, wenn sie denn fantasievoll integriert sind in die Erlebnisfolge des Parkbesuchs.

Eine einzigartige Skateanlage, ein Trampolinparcours oder überdimensionale Reckstangen laden ein, sich sportlich zu messen, wirkliche Herausforderungen zu bestehen. Und genau das wollen Jugendliche heute im Park, daher gehen sie in den Park. Wenn man für solche Angebote Ideen und Mittel aufbringt, sind plötzlich alle dabei, es entsteht das gemeinsame Erfolgserlebnis.

Man muss die Leute von zu Hause weglocken, und das geht heute nur mit herausragenden Angeboten. Und entsprechendem finanziellen Aufwand. *Dafür* müssen Gelder für die Parks zur Verfügung stehen.

Der gesellschaftliche Aufwand für einen Park ist erheblich, doch ist er auch begründet? Warum ist dieses In-den-Park-Gehen gesellschaftlich so bedeutsam?

CG: Park soll Raum für Aneignungen sein. Entsprechend muss auch das logistische Angebot, die Ausstattung eines Parks mit Wegen, WCs und vielem Weiteren angelegt sein. Und wenn eine intensive Nutzung einsetzt, kann es nicht Ziel sein, diese zu regulieren, sondern man muss dann eben die Infrastruktur anpassen, damit man sich alltags wie sonntags dort wohlfühlt. Ein Park muss immer auch robust und veränderbar sein.

Can landscape architecture compete with the intensity and diversity of experience offered by the virtual world?

CG: More to the point, Being in the park means offering parallel worlds. Things can take place in the park that can't take place elsewhere. I once re-edited film sequences from scenes taking place in parks, from *Hair* to *Gorky Park* to Paul Auster's *Manhattan Stories*. A park is always a space that exists in contrast to the normal world. The park must at least allow the experience of parallel worlds. At best it should stimulate people to move from contemplation to action.

In this respect the spring garden in the Gardens of the World triggers a very different heart rate than climbing up to the Wolkenhain would. Or the volcanoes in Schwerin, with their 7 metre height – a huge challenge for children.

KH: Special features in terms of colour, form and size are part and parcel of a good park for us. However, retro features also have an appeal and give pleasure when they are imaginatively integrated into the experience of a visit to the park.

A unique skate park, a trampoline course or oversized horizontal bars invite visitors to test their sporting skills, to take on real challenges. And this is precisely what young people want today. That's why they go to the park. If we produce the ideas and materials to offer this, suddenly everyone is on board, experiencing a shared sense of achievement.

You have to entice people out of their houses, and that is only possible today if you offer something excellent. This requires the corresponding financial scope. For this reason, money must be available for parks.

The social cost for a park is considerable, yet is it also justified? Why is this Being in the park socially significant?

CG: A park should be a space for appropriation. Correspondingly, the logistics aspect – equipment in the park such as paths, WCs and much more – must be created. And when it is used frequently, the aim cannot be to regulate these. The infrastructure then simply has to be adjusted so that people feel at home there every day as well as on Sundays. Among other things, a park must always be robust and modifiable.

Skateanlage im Felsenmeer, Hemer

Skate Park in Felsenmeer, Hemer

KH: Es geht um ein gemeinsames Forum für alle Menschen. Und das kann nur der Park sein, nicht die Schule, nicht der Garten, nicht die Alteneinrichtung. Wo soll Austausch sonst passieren, wenn nicht im öffentlichen Raum? Das macht den Park gesellschaftlich so bedeutsam.
Ungezwungener Aufenthalt ist wichtig für die Entwicklung des Menschen, für sein Wohlbefinden. Wir brauchen Orte, die Alternativen bieten zum Stillsitzen, zum dauernd Gefordertsein. Freiraum eben. Sich auslassen, sich erholen, alle viere von sich strecken, abreagieren, in der Sonne sitzen: alles ungezwungene, nicht eingezwängte Alternativen zum vorgeprägten Alltag – und das alles kann man im Park besser als andernorts. Und daher sind Parks eine soziale Verantwortung.

Aussichtsplatz Himmelstreppe, Hemer

Observation Platform Stairway to Heaven, Hemer

CG: Eine soziale Verantwortung für den Raum. Ein Park stiftet Identität, erzeugt Stolz bei den Anwohnern. Stolz, weil sich eine Kommune einen Park leistet, obwohl der ja aus der typischen Verwertungsökonomie herausfällt. Das stärkt die Identifizierung mit der eigenen Gemeinde und damit die Bürgerschaft. Die dann wieder bereit ist, der Stadt ihr Engagement zu geben. Ein Park gibt einer Gesellschaft Ausdruck, bringt die Bürger zum Sprechen.

Wird anhand der Parks die gesellschaftliche Identität der jeweiligen Stadt verhandelt?

CG: Ja, ganz eindeutig. Nehmen wir Hemer, die durch Militär und Metallindustrie geprägte Stadt im Sauerland, wobei beides vor Ort keine große Bedeutung, keine große Zukunft mehr hatte. Wenn die Stadt heute aufgrund des Parks nun zu vielen Veranstaltungen einlädt, stolzer Gastgeber ist, prägt das die gesellschaftliche Identität.

KH: Wir versuchen uns einen Eindruck zu verschaffen von der jeweiligen sozialen Identität der Stadt, in der ein Park liegt. Wenn man die Nutzungen analysiert, sich einige Tage in oder am Rande einer Parkanlage aufhält, erfährt man fast alles über Spannungen und Erwartungen in einer Stadt.

ERZÄHLUNGEN IM PARK

Wie wird in den Parks dann diese Geschichte der Stadt erzählt?

KH: Die gesteigerte Intensität des Erlebens – die Höhepunkte der Anlagen, wo sich Menschen im Erlebnis, im Spiel

KH: It is about a joint forum for everyone. And that is something only a park can do. Not a school, a garden, or a nursing home. Where is exchange to take place if not in the public space? This is what makes parks so socially significant.
Casually spending time somewhere is important for human development, for people's well-being. We need places that offer alternatives to sitting still, to being constantly under pressure. Simply open space. Let yourself go, relax, stretch out, work it all off, sit in the sun: unforced rather than forced alternatives to everyday life – and all this can be done in the park in a better way than anywhere else. And parks are therefore a social responsibility.

CG: A space-related social responsibility. A park creates an identity, generates pride among the residents. There is pride in the fact that the municipality can afford a park, although parks are not typically included under commercial economies. This strengthens people's identification with their own municipality and with the citizenry. This makes them willing to once again engage with the city. A park gives expression to society and gets the citizens talking.

Is the social identity of the specific city negotiated on the basis of the park?

CG: : Yes, quite clearly. Let's take Hemer, a city in Sauerland characterised by the military and the metal industry. With neither playing any role there, it had no

treffen – ist eine Besonderheit unserer Arbeit. Voraussetzung dafür ist das Einfühlen in die unterschiedlichen Interessen und Generationen der Parkbesucher. Das speist sich natürlich immer auch aus persönlichen Interessen und Einflüssen.

CG: Manche unserer Entwürfe folgen einfach dem eigenen Spaß, ganz frei von Untersuchungen und Analysen. Daraus können dann wiederum Vorbilder entstehen.

Parks, speziell auch Gartenschauen, bieten immer wieder die Chance, auch einmal etwas völlig Neues zu entwickeln. Da macht es dann Spaß, an einigen Stellen einfach mal barock zu werden, alle Sinne zugleich anzusprechen, einfach mal über die Stränge zu schlagen – und wir zeigen damit auch, wie eine klimaresiliente Stadt der Zukunft aussehen könnte.

Der Park ist nicht so sehr das von uns Landschaftsarchitekten vorgegebene Drehbuch. Die Erzählung entsteht vielmehr durch die Menschen, die sich im Park im Erlebnis treffen. Also nicht wir als Landschaftsarchitekten erzählen eine Geschichte mittels eines Parks, sondern wir bringen Rahmen, Figuren und Handlungsideen ein; und die Geschichte(n) erzählen dann diejenigen, die sich mit ganz unterschiedlichen Erwartungen im Park treffen.

Also wird in unserer Entwurfsarbeit nicht die einfache Dialektik aus Erzähler und Empfänger kultiviert, sondern Geschichten werden erzählt aus dem Erlebnis des Parks heraus, weil die Landschaftsarchitektur zu diesen Erlebnissen anregt. Die Landschaftsarchitektur bietet also nicht die Erzählung, sondern die Erzählanlässe. Im Park entstehen Erzählungen.

real future. Today, the city issues invitations to many events thanks to the park. This makes it the proud host, and this defines its social identity.

KH: We try to get an impression of the specific social identity of the city in which the park is located. If we analyse the usages and stay for some days in or at the edge of the park complex, we can find out everything about the tensions and expectations in a city.

TALES IN THE PARK

How is this story of the city then told in the parks?

KH: The increased intensity of experience – the highlights of the facilities where people meet to experience things and to play – is a special feature of our work. The prerequisite for this is empathising with the various interests and the different generations of park visitors. Naturally, this always derives from personal interests and influences.

CG: Some of our designs simply follow our own fun, quite free from investigations and analyses. This can then produce new models.

Parks, and especially garden exhibitions, repeatedly offer the opportunity to develop something completely new for once. It's fun to simply be baroque in some places, to address all the senses at the same time and to simply run riot for once. In doing so, we also demonstrate what a climate resilient city of the future could look like.

The park is not really a screenplay specified by us landscape architects. Rather, the narrative originates from the people who meet in the park for the sake of experiences. Therefore it is not the landscape architects who tell a story through a park. Instead, we provide a framework, figures and ideas for activities; and the stories are then told by those who meet in the park, with all their very different expectations.

Therefore, in our design work it is not the simple dialectic of storyteller and recipient that is cultivated. Instead, stories arise from what has been experienced in the park because landscape architecture stimulates these experiences. Thus, landscape architecture does not offer the narrative itself, but the reason for the narrative. Narratives originate in the park.

Erholung in den Gärten der Welt, Berlin

Relaxation in the Gardens of the World, Berlin

KIENBERGPARK BERLIN

Transformation Landschaft

Transformation Landscape

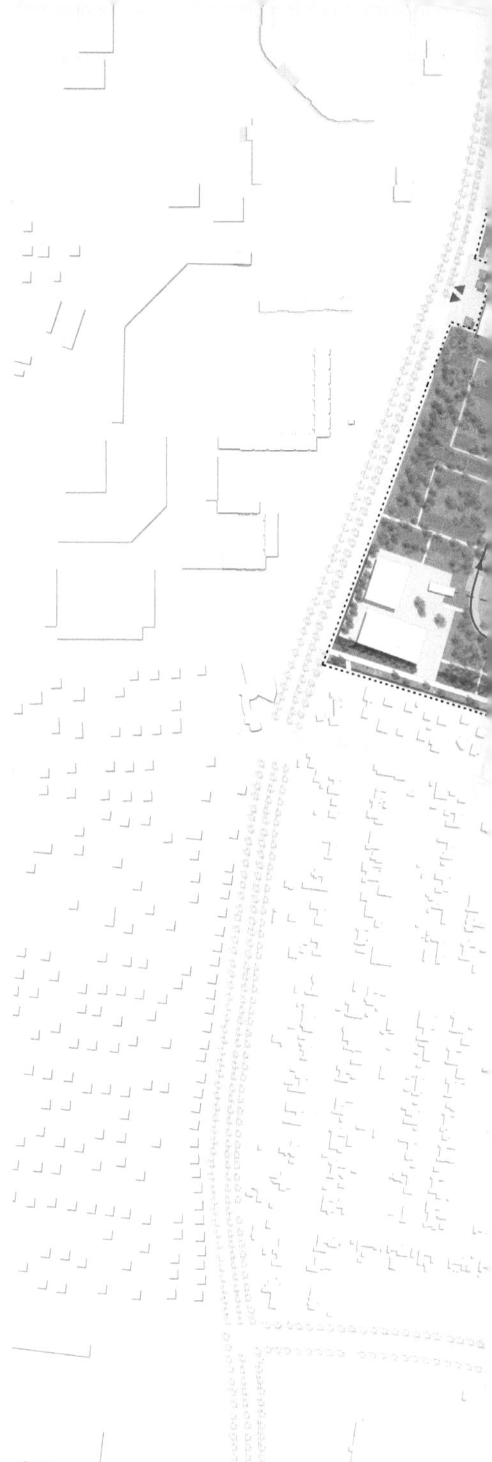

Bereits von Weitem ist der Kienberg über der Großsiedlung Marzahn-Hellersdorf zu erkennen. Als zentraler Bezugspunkt im Wuhletal gibt dieser aus Trümmern und Bauschutt geformte Berg dem Park seinen Namen. Mit dem Kienbergpark ist im Zuge der IGA Berlin 2017 ein 64 Hektar großer, zeitgenössischer öffentlicher Landschaftspark mit einigen herausragenden Folies entstanden. Dieser Landschaftspark der Gegenwart lädt ein zu einer Entdeckungsreise mit zahlreichen Bewegungsangeboten, aber auch zur ruhigen Erholung und zum Naturerleben an der städtischen Peripherie. Intensiv gestaltete Zonen wechseln sich mit großen, extensiv gestalteten Bereichen des Naturerlebnisses ab.

The Kienberg can be seen from afar, rising above the large housing estate of Marzahn-Hellersdorf. This hill formed from rubble and construction waste gives the park its name. It is a central reference point in the Wuhle Valley. Kienberg Park is a 64-hectare, contemporary public landscape park with some excellent backdrops. This park was created for the International Garden Show Berlin 2017. This contemporary landscape park of the present invites visitors to take a voyage of discovery, offing plenty of options for keeping fit, but also the chance to enjoy peaceful recreation and to experience nature on the urban periphery. Intensely designed zones alternate with large, extensively designed areas for experiencing nature.

Internationale Gartenausstellung Berlin 2017
Erweiterung Gärten der Welt und Kienbergpark

Leistungszeitraum: 2014–2017
Partner: Kolb Ripke Gesellschaft von Architekten mbH Berlin und VIC Planen und Beraten GmbH Potsdam
Leistungsphasen: 1–9
Fläche: 64 Hektar

International Garden Exhibition Berlin 2017
Extension Gardens of the World and Kienberg Park

Construction Period 2014–2017
Partners: Kolb Ripke Gesellschaft von Architekten mbH Berlin VIC Planen and Beraten GmbH Potsdam
Construction Phases: 1–9
Area: 64 hectares

Haupteingang,
Gärten der Welt, Berlin

Main Entrance,
Gardens of the World, Berlin

Seilbahn zum Kienberg

Cable Railway to Kienberg

KIENBERG

Von seinem Haupteingang auf Höhe des U-Bahnhofes Kienbergpark (Gärten der Welt) leitet der Park den Besucher über die Kienbergpromenade in die sogenannten Gärten der Welt, wo sich seit den 1990er Jahren eine wachsende Anzahl Gartenkulturen aus aller Welt präsentiert. Über die Seilbahn und den Wuhlesteg verbindet der Kienbergpark die Stadtteile Marzahn und Hellersdorf.

Für Berliner Verhältnisse ist der Kienberg mit seinen 102 Metern über Normalnull, eine stattliche Anhöhe. Sie hat einen eiszeitlichen Ursprung, wuchs aber durch Trümmerschutt nach dem Zweiten Weltkrieg und später durch Bauaushub der umliegenden Neubausiedlungen auf fast die doppelte Höhe an. Mit der skulpturalen Aussichtsplattform Wolkenhain (Kolb Ripke Architekten) „wächst" der Kienberg um nochmals 20 Meter nach oben. Die neue Terrassierung des Südhangs betont die künstliche Entstehung des Kienbergs, der durch die verschiedenen Aufschüttungen das Profil eines Tafelbergs hat.

KIENBERG

From its main entrance, which is on a level with the Kienberg Park (Gardens of the World) underground station, the park guides the visitor over the Kienberg promenade to the Gardens of the World, to which a growing number of garden cultures from all over the world have been introduced since the 1990s. Kienberg Park is linked to the districts of Marzahn and Hellersdorf via the cable railway and Wuhle Bridge.

From Berlin's view, the Kienberg has an impressive height, rising 102 metres above sea level. Its origins lie in the ice age; however, it was raised to almost double its height by the addition of rubble after the Second World War, and later through the excavation for the surrounding new housing estate. With the sculptured observation platform Wolkenhain (Kolb Ripke Architects), the Kienberg is "growing" upwards once again by 20 metres. The new terracing of the southern slope emphasises the artificial emergence of the Kienberg;

Alle neu eingefügten Architekturen – neben dem Wolkenhain und den Kienbergterrassen bereichern die Zwischenstation der Seilbahn, die neue Tälchenbrücke sowie Spiel- und Sportangebote den Kienberg – treten in einen spannungsreichen Dialog mit der Natur, die sich waldartig über den Trümmerschutt gelegt hat. Der bestehende Jungwaldcharakter des Kienbergs bildete den Ausgangspunkt für dessen Gestaltung und ökologische Weiterentwicklung. Auf der Grundlage des Pflege- und Entwicklungsplanes für den Kienberg und das Wuhletal, der zusammen mit Naturschutzverbänden erarbeitet wurde, entstanden als ein Beitrag zur Förderung der biologischen Vielfalt unterschiedliche Lebensräume für Pflanzen und Tiere. Waldbereiche, in denen die in Berlin typischen Baumarten Eiche, Buche, Birke und Kiefer gepflanzt werden, wechseln sich mit Waldsäumen und hellen, sonnigen Lichtungen ab. Landschaftsarchitekten haben hier eine Waldentwicklung im Sinne einer großen Vielfalt an zukünftigen Waldbildern initiiert.

Auch die architektonisch geprägten Kienbergterrassen mit ihren blühenden Staudenpflanzungen leisten einen Beitrag zur biologischen Vielfalt. Die Trockensteinmauern, aus denen die Terrassen geformt sind, bieten unter anderem der Zauneidechse einen Unterschlupf, einer heute fast überall gefährdeten Art.

Der Südwesthang des Kienbergs mit vielfältigen Blicken auf Hellersdorf ist als Obstbaumwiese gestaltet. Mit ihren historischen und selten gewordenen Obstgehölzen – unterschiedliche Apfel- und Birnensorten, Quitten, Pflaumen und Kirschen – sowie mit blühenden Wiesenkräutern bildet sie eine Lebensgrundlage für Bienen, Käfer, Schmetterlinge, Vögel, aber auch kleine Säugetiere. Für die Umsetzung des Obstbaumhanges kooperierten die Landschaftsarchitekten mit dem Landesverband Berlin der Gartenfreunde e.V., der Allianz Umweltstiftung, der Stiftung NatureLife-International sowie mit den Marzahner Gartenfreunden der benachbarten Kleingartenanlage Am Kienberg.

KIENBERGPROMENADE UND KIENBERGTERRASSEN

Die Kienbergpromenade verläuft in Verlängerung des Beltwalks aus den Gärten der Welt in zwei Höhenstufen entlang des Südhangs. Sie führt barrierefrei über die Obstwiesen zu den Kienbergterrassen, die den Hang mit sorgsam geschichteten Trockensteinmauern aus dunkelgrauem Theumaer Fruchtschiefer gliedern. Über 20 Meter ziehen sich die Terrassen am Hang hoch, verbunden über Stufen und Rampen. Einige Terrassenfelder sind als „Steinbilder" gestaltet.

the various infills have given it the profile of a table mountain.

All the newly introduced items of architecture – besides the Wolkenhain and the Kienberg terraces, Kienberg has been enriched by the intermediate station of the cable railway, the new little valley bridge and facilities for sport and play – enter into an exciting dialogue with the nature that has covered the rubble like a forest. The existing young forest character of the Kienberg formed the starting point for the design and the ecological further development project. An initiative for promoting the biological diversity of different habitats for plants and animals emerged based on the management and development plan for the Kienberg and Wuhle valley that was developed together with nature conservation societies. Forest areas planted with typical Berlin tree species (oak, beech, birch, and pine), alternate with forest borders and bright, sunny clearings. Here, landscape architects have initiated a forest development geared to producing a great diversity of future forest profiles.

The Kienberg terraces, with their architectural character and blossoming plantation of shrubs, also contribute to biological diversity. The drystone walls from which the terraces are formed offer refuge to species that include the sand lizard, today a widely endangered species.

The southwest slope of the Kienberg, which offers a wide range of views over Hellersdorf, is designed as an orchard. Its historic and rare fruit trees – a wide variety of apples and pears, quince, plums and cherries – join with blossoming meadow herbs to form the basis of existence for bees, beetles, butterflies, and birds, but also small mammals. To create the fruit tree slope, the landscape architects cooperated with the state association Berlin der Gartenfreunde e.V., Allianz Umweltstiftung, the foundation NatureLife-International, and the Marzahn Gartenfreunden from the neighbouring allotment gardens Am Kienberg.

KIENBERG PROMENADE AND KIENBERG TERRACES

The Kienberg promenade runs along the belt walk from the Gardens of the World along the southern slope, at two height levels. With no barriers, it leads over the orchard to the Kienberg terraces, which divide up the slope with carefully layered drystone

Kienbergterrassen
Kienberg Terraces

Die vier Terrassenfelder bieten Sitzgelegenheiten, um den Blick in das Tal zu genießen, durch das sich der Biesdorf-Marzahner Grenzgraben schlängelt.

Einen anderen, direkten und sportlichen Weg auf den Berg bietet der Kienbergsteig, eine Treppenanlage, die von den Kienbergterrassen fast geradlinig hinauf zur Bergkuppe und zum Wolkenhain führt.

KONRAD BEI DEN POLYNESISCHEN RIESENAMEISEN

Unterhalb des Wolkenhains am Kienberg begegnet man auf einer Waldlichtung polynesischen Riesenameisen, von denen Konrad, der neunjährige Held aus Erich Kästners Kinderbuch *Der 35. Mai oder Konrad reitet in die Südsee,* im Urwald überrascht wird. 7 Meter lange und 3 Meter hohe Ameisen scheinen mitten am Kienberg auf einen zuzukommen. Die langbeinigen Tiere sind als Gruppe zu einem großen Klettergerüst montiert. Dazu gibt es einen riesigen „Ameisenhaufen" aus Holz und Stahl, den man ebenfalls erklettern kann. Der Spielplatz geht ohne Begrenzungen über in die naturnahe Umgebung, sodass der Wald ins Spiel einbezogen werden kann. Für die Großen bietet sich von der Waldlichtung aus ein beeindruckender Blick über die Gärten der Welt.

Ein weiterer Spielplatz, „Konrad in Elektropolis", wurde gemeinsam mit Jugendlichen aus der Nachbarschaft entwickelt, die in einer Werkstatt ihre Wünsche für diesen „Spielplatz von morgen" einbrachten. Wer hat eigentlich das Mobiltelefon erfunden? In seiner Fantasie von 1931 stellte sich Erich Kästner „Manteltaschentelefone" vor ebenso wie selbstfahrende Autos und künstliche Gärten. All dies bestaunt Konrad, der neunjährige Held der Geschichte, in der automatisierten Zukunftsstadt Elektropolis, die die Anregung für die Ausgestaltung dieses Spielplatzes gab. Auf 1800 Quadratmetern finden vor allem ältere Kinder und Jugendliche vielfältige Angebote zum Klettern, Rutschen, Springen, Skaten oder Chillen. Eingebettet in eine modellierte Asphaltfläche liegt ein technoid anmutender Kletterturm, auf dem man sich bis in 8 Meter Höhe wagen kann. Die gestapelten und miteinander verbundenen Würfel erinnern an die Wolkenkratzer in Elektropolis. Trampoline, Hängematten und Sitzbänke bieten Möglichkeiten, sich zu bewegen und zu entspannen.

Die Spielplätze, die gestalterisch der Geschichte Erich Kästners folgen und durch das Rollschuhpferd als wiederkehrendes Element erzählerisch wie gestalterisch verbunden sind, sind auch im Kienbergpark eine Attraktion und

walls made of dark grey Theuma coloured slate. The terraces ascend up the slope by more than 20 metres. They are linked by steps and ramps. Some terrace fields are designed as "stone scenes". The four terrace fields provide seating so that visitors can enjoy the view of the valley and of the Biesdorf-Marzahn boundary ditch that winds through it.

The Kienbergsteig offers an alternative direct (and sporty) way up the hill. It is a stairway that travels almost all the way to the mountain top in a straight line from the Kienberg terraces and leads to the Wolkenhain.

KONRAD WITH THE POLYNESIAN GIANT ANTS

In a clearing in the woods below the Wolkenhain on the Kienberg, we encounter Polynesian giant ants startling Konrad, the nine-year-old hero from Erich Kästner's children's book *Der 35. Mai oder Konrad reitet in die Südsee,* in the jungle. In the middle of Kienberg, one is apparently approached by 7-metre-long and 3-metre-high ants. The long-legged animals are assembled as a group, forming one large climbing frame. There is a giant "anthill" made of wood and steel that you can also climb up. The play-ground transitions into the natural environment without any boundaries, so that the forest can be included in any play. The "adults" can enjoy an impres-sive view over the Gardens of the World from the clearing in the woods.

Another playground, "Konrad in Electropolis", was developed together with young people from the neighbourhood, who introduced their ideas for this "playground of tomorrow" to the workshop. Who really invented the mobile telephone? In his 1931 fantasy, Erich Kästner imagined "coat pocket telephones", along with self-driving cars and artificial gardens. As the nine-year-old hero of the story in the automated future city of Electropolis, Konrad marvelled at all this; this provided the idea behind the design of this playground. Over an area of 1,800 square metres, older children and young people in particular find a wide range of opportunities to climb, slide, jump, skate, or chill. Embedded in a modelled asphalt area is a seemingly technoid climbing tower on which you can venture up to 8 metres in height. The stacked and linked dice bring to mind the skyscrapers of Electropolis.

Spielplatz „Konrad bei den Polinesischen Riesenameisen"
Playground "Konrad with the Polynesian Giant Ants"

unterstreichen, warum geskes.hack die Erfahrung des Raumes im Spiel so wichtig ist. „Das Spiel ermöglicht Begegnung, Kommunikation, Ins-Gespräch-Kommen", betonen die Landschaftsarchitekten. Diesem Schlüssel des Parkerlebens widmen sie daher immer wieder besondere Aufmerksamkeit, ob nun dem überraschenden Maßstabssprung durch die Größe der tierischen Objekte, die schon in der Geschichte Kästners angelegt ist, oder durch die besondere Sorgfalt in der Auswahl der Materialien und Farben. Wer durch die Darmzotten des riesigen Wals kriecht, nimmt diese Leidenschaft für die Inszenierung bis ins Detail wahr.

TÄLCHENBRÜCKE

Die Tälchenbrücke (Kolb Ripke Architekten) verbindet ein Plateau auf halber Höhe des Kienbergs mit den Gärten der Welt. Klar und geradlinig zieht sich die 85 Meter lange Brücke aus rostrotem Cortenstahl über das „Tälchen". Die Brücke führt zu einem als Marzahner Ausguck bekannten Hügel. Von diesem Aussichtsplateau, das von niedrigen Mauern gerahmt und mit Sitzgelegenheiten ausgestattet ist, gelangt man, vorbei am Christlichen Garten oder dem Karl-Foerster-Garten, ins Innere der Gärten der Welt.

Mit ihrer Konstruktion als Trogsteg und dem Cortenstahl als Material gleicht die Tälchenbrücke dem Wuhlesteg. Diese Verwandtschaft kommt nicht von ungefähr: Die Tälchenbrücke stammt von denselben Architekten und

Trampolines, hammocks, and benches provide opportunities to move around and to relax.

The playgrounds whose designs are based on the stories of Erich Kästner – connected in terms of narrative and design by the recurring element of the horse on roller-skates – are also an attraction for Kienberg Park. They underline why geskes.hack consider the experience of space in play to be so important. The landscape architects emphasise that "play enables movement, communication, getting into conversation". They therefore pay special attention to this key aspect of the park experience; this can be seen in the surprising jump in scale created by the size of the animal objects (anchored in Kästner's story) or due to the special care in the choice of materials and colours. Anyone who walks through the intestinal villi of the giant whale will be aware of this passion for the proper staging of everything, down to the last detail.

LITTLE VALLEY BRIDGE

The little valley bridge links a plateau halfway up the Kienberg with the Gardens of the World. This 85-metre long bridge made of rust-red Corten steel stretches clearly and in a straight line over the "little valley". The bridge leads to a hill known as the Marzahn Lookout. From this observation plateau, which is framed by low walls and furnished with seating, one reaches the

Tälchenbrücke, Verbindung des Kienbergs zu den Gärten der Welt

Little Valley Bridge links Kienberg to the Gardens of the World

Wuhlesteg zum Kienbergpark
Wuhle Bridge to Kienberg Park

Wuhlesteg, Richtung Hellersdorf

Wuhle Bridge in the Direction of Hellersdorf

stellt ganz bewusst nicht nur räumlich, sondern auch in der Gestaltsprache eine Verbindung zwischen den Gärten der Welt und dem Kienbergpark her. Und unterstreicht so ein Entwurfsprinzip, nämlich architektonisch-ingenieurstechnische Elemente in den künstlichen Naturraum des Kienbergparks kontrastreich zu integrieren.

WUHLESTEG UND WUHLETEICH

Auen- und Wiesenlandschaften sowie kleinere, überwiegend künstlich angelegte Gewässer wie der Wuhleteich prägen die eiszeitliche Rinne des Wuhletals im Bereich des Kienbergparks. Das Areal ist mit seinen neu angelegten Flachwasserzonen eine abwechslungsreiche Naturerlebniszone mit ihrer spezifischen Tier- und Pflanzenwelt, beispielsweise dem Eisvogel.

280 Meter weit spannt sich der Wuhlesteg (Kolb Ripke Architekten) über das Wuhletal. Ausgehend vom Jelena-Šantić-Friedenspark quert der Steg aus Cortenstahl zunächst den Wuhletal-Rad-/Wanderweg. Er fällt dann ab

inside of the Gardens of the World, passing the Christian Garden or the Karl-Foerster-Garden.

The trough footbridge construction and the Corten steel material make the little valley bridge similar to the Wuhle Bridge. This affinity has not sprung out of nowhere: the little valley bridge was created by the same architects and very consciously makes a connection not only spatially but also in the design language between the Gardens of the World and Kienberg Park. In doing so, it underlines the design principle by integrating architectural and engineering elements into the artificial natural space of Kienberg Park in a richly contrasting way.

WUHLE BRIDGE AND WUHLE POND

The ice-age channels of the Wuhle Valley in the Kienberg Park area are characterised by pasture and meadow landscapes, as well as smaller and primarily artificially created bodies of water like Wuhle Pond.

und führt entlang des nördlichen Ufers des Wuhleteichs flach über Wiesen und wechselfeuchte Bereiche bis zum Fuß des Kienbergs. Hier endet er an der scheinbar schwebenden Holzplattform der Seeterrasse. Der Steg schafft eine neue Verbindung zwischen den Ortsteilen Marzahn und Hellersdorf. Unterbrochen wird die schlichte Trogkonstruktion aus Cortenstahl von einem transparenten Balkon. Im Umweltbildungszentrum am Wuhleteich werden die Besonderheiten dieses stadtnahen Naturraums vor allem Kindern und Jugendlichen vermittelt. Ein Ort für das gezielte Entdecken.

BELVEDERE AM HAUPTEINGANG KIENBERGPARK

1200 junge Birken flankieren den Haupteingang zum Kienbergpark am U-Bahnhof Kienbergpark (Gärten der Welt). Als ein filigraner grüner Mantel legt sich diese Pflanzung um den Parkeingang und schirmt ihn gegenüber Straße und Wohngebiet ab. Vom Kienberg über den Wuhlesteg kommend, empfängt die Besucher zunächst das Belvedere.

Diese „schöne Aussicht" – so die wörtliche Übersetzung aus dem Italienischen – schafft einen Ruhepol am Haupteingang des Kienbergparks und betont eine stadt- und landschaftsräumlich herausragende Situation. Der Blick folgt der neuen „Stadtspange", der mit der IGA 2017 entstandenen Grünverbindung zwischen Hellersdorf und Marzahn. Kienberg, Wuhle und Wuhleteich, der Wuhlesteg, die Seilbahn und das Umweltbildungszentrum liegen innerhalb des Panoramas. So empfängt das Belvedere die Besucher mit einer weiten Aussicht – oder entlässt sie, vom Kienberg kommend, mit einem abschließenden Blick.

WOLKENHAIN

Auf einer Wolke schweben – wer hat davon nicht schon einmal geträumt? Auf einer Wolke immerhin spazieren und über den Bäumen schweben kann man in Berlin auf dem Kienbergplateau. Mit der spektakulären skulpturalen Aussichtsplattform Wolkenhain gelang den Architekten Kolb Ripke ein außergewöhnliches Werk der Ingenieurs- und Architekturkunst. Gemeinsam mit geskes.hack setzten sich die Architekten auch aufgrund dieses Bauwerks im landschaftsarchitektonischen Wettbewerb zur Gestaltung des Kienbergparks durch.

Die poetische Konstruktion entstand aus dem Gedanken, dass man losgelöst von der vertrauten Umgebung hoch über dem Kienberg schweben können müsste, um

The area is a varied nature experience zone with its newly designed flat water zones featuring their own specific world of plants and animals, such as the kingfishers.

The Wuhle Bridge spans 280 metres over the Wuhle Valley. Starting from the Jelena-Šantić-Friedenspark (the Jelena-Šantić Peace Park), this bridge made from Corten steel initially crosses the Wuhle Valley cycle and hiking path. It then descends, running level along the northern bank of the Wuhle Pond over meadows and semi-humid areas to the foot of Kienberg. It ends here at the seemingly hovering wooden platform of the lake terrace. The bridge creates a new link between the districts of Marzahn and Hellersdorf. The simple support structure made of Corten steel is interrupted by a transparent balcony. The Centre for Environmental Education at the Wuhle Pond provides information about the special features of this natural space close to the city, especially for children and young people. This is a place for purposeful discovery.

BELVEDERE AT THE MAIN ENTRANCE TO KIENBERG PARK

1,200 young birch trees flank the main entrance to Kienberg Park at the Kienberg Park (Gardens of the World) underground station. These plants surround the park entrance like a delicate green coat and shield it from the street and residential area. The Belvedere initially welcomes the visitors coming from Kienberg to the Wuhle Bridge.

This "beautiful view" – the literal translation of the Italian word "belvedere" – creates a haven of peace at the main entrance of Kienberg Park and highlights an outstanding urban and rural setting. The view follows the new "city clasp": the green connection between Hellersdorf and Marzahn originating from the International Garden Exhibition 2017. Kienberg, Wuhle and Wuhle Pond, Wuhle Bridge, the cable railway, and the Centre for Environmental Education are located within the panorama. Thus, the Belvedere welcomes visitors with a wide view – or bids them farewell, if they are coming from Kienberg, with a final view.

WOLKENHAIN

Hovering on a cloud – who hasn't dreamt of this at one time or another? At any rate, one can walk on a cloud

Hellersdorfer Fenster am Wuhletal
Hellersdorf Window at Wuhle Valley

Märkischer Garten
Märkischer Garden

den Panoramablick bis ins Berliner Stadtzentrum und ins Brandenburgische genießen zu können. Der Zugang zu der Aussichtsplattform „windet" sich in Fortsetzung des Spazierweges vom Kienbergplateau auf etwa 130 Metern über Normalnull in die Höhe.

Die schlanken Stützen des Wolkenhains zitieren die umgebenden Baumstämme, sie bilden den „Hain". Über eine Treppenanlage, alternativ per Aufzug, erreicht man die Höhe der „Wolke", die als unregelmäßig ausgeformter Steg einen Rundparcours bildet. Von hier aus blickt man über das Wuhletal bis zum Müggelturm in Köpenick, über Hellersdorf, über die Gärten der Welt nach Marzahn und bis in das Stadtzentrum Berlins.

Die Konstruktion besteht aus ca. 170 Stahlknoten, die die Verstrebungen der Wolke zusammenhalten. Die Unterkonstruktion des Aussichtsstegs ist von einer weißen, transluzenten Folie umhüllt, woraus die eigentliche Wolkenskulptur entsteht. Sie bildet zusammen mit dem Kienberg eine weithin erkennbare Landmarke. Die Wolke wird dezent von innen illuminiert. Der programmierbare Farbverlauf kann dem natürlichen Licht folgen, aber auch bewusst konträr dazu wirken und passt sich dem jeweiligen Tageslichtniveau an oder zeigt in der Nacht besondere Akzente.

ERSCHLIESSUNG

Die Erschließung des Kienberggeländes ist bewusst sehr unterschiedlich gestaltet. Sie erfolgt über den Hellersdorfer Weg, einen grob geschotterten Waldweg, den Tälchenweg, den steilen Kienbergsteig, die Kienbergpromenade als Teil einer neuen Stadtspange Marzahn-Hellersdorf und einer schnellen Radwegverbindung sowie über den Weg des Wolkenhains und ist eine besondere planerische Leistung von geskes.hack Landschaftsarchitekten. Darin kommt die Diversität des Geländes ebenso zum Ausdruck wie die Bedeutung der städtebaulichen Bezüge. Eine weitere Besonderheit ist die Seilbahn, die über dem Landschaftspark schwebt. Um das über 56 Hektar große Gelände des Kienbergparks barrierefrei zu erreichen und an den U-Bahnhof Kienbergpark (Gärten der Welt) anzubinden, erwies sich die Seilbahn-Technik als umweltverträglichste Variante der Verkehrserschließung.

Die Seilbahnstrecke verläuft auf 1,5 Kilometern zwischen der Station Gärten der Welt am Blumberger Damm, der Station auf dem Kienbergplateau unweit des Wolkenhains und der Station Kienbergpark im südwestlichen Teil des Areals. Die Fahrt in bis zu 30 Metern Höhe dauert

and hover over the trees on the Kienberg plateau in Berlin. In the spectacular Wolkenhain sculptural observation platform, the architect Kolb Ripke has succeeded in creating an exceptional engineering and architectural work of art. The architect also succeeded in winning the landscape architecture competition (jointly with geskes.hack) to design Kienberg Park based on this structure.

The poetic construction stemmed from the idea that one would have to hover high above the Kienberg – released from the familiar environment – to enjoy the panoramic view over Berlin's city centre and Brandenburg. The entrance to the observation platform "winds", continuing the walking route from the Kienberg plateau to around 130 metres above sea level.

The slender columns of the Wolkenhain echo the surrounding tree trunks, forming a "grove". One reaches the level of the "cloud", which forms a circular course designed as an irregularly shaped bridge, via a stairway (or alternatively by elevator). From here visitors can enjoy a view over the Wuhle Valley all the way to the Müggel Tower in Köpenick over Hellersdorf to the Gardens of the World to Marzahn and to the city centre of Berlin.

The construction comprises approx. 170 steel knots that hold the braces of the cloud together. The substructure of the viewing bridge is wrapped in a white, translucent foil, which constitutes the actual cloud sculpture. Together with the Kienberg, it forms a landmark that can be seen from afar. The cloud is discreetly illuminated from the inside. The programmable colour gradient can follow the natural light, but can also consciously appear contrary to it, and can adjust to the respective daylight level or shows special accentuations at night.

DEVELOPMENT

The development of the Kienberg site was intentionally designed in a very varied way. It proceeds via the Hellersdorfer Weg, a roughly gravelled forest path, the little valley path, the steep Kienberg climb, the Kienberg promenade (as part of a new Marzahn-Hellersdorf city clasp) and a quick cycle route link, as well as via the path of the Wolkenhain. This is a special planning achievement by geskes.hack Landscape Architects.

It expresses the diversity of the site as well as the significance of the urban references. Another special

Aussichtsplattform Wolkenhain

Observation Platform Wolkenhain

insgesamt 5 Minuten. Pro Stunde kann die Seilbahn bis zu 3000 Fahrgäste aufnehmen, die den Blick aus der Vogelperspektive genießen.

Die drei Seilbahnstationen sind aus einem einzigen Entwurf der Architekten Kolb Ripke heraus entstanden. Als „grüne Welle", die sich aus dem Boden heraus- und über den Kienberg wieder hinunterschwingt, sind die Gebäude mit ihren begrünten Dächern ein Teil der Landschaft.

Der Wiesenhang am westlichen Kienberg ist durch eine Veranstaltungsarena, ein Besucherzentrum für die Gärten der Welt und den Kienbergpark, durch einen großen Wasserspielplatz und vor allem durch die Wassergärten markiert. Bevor man es sieht, hört man: Wasser. Es rauscht, plätschert, sprudelt. Die Wasserwelten im Kienbergpark sind Gartenkabinette, in denen vielfältige Erscheinungsformen des Wassers stimmungsvoll inszeniert werden. Wie an einer Perlenschnur aufgereiht liegen die Wassergärten unterhalb des Beltwalk. Dieser führt durch weite Parkwiesen südlich am Fuß des Kienbergs entlang bis zu den Gärten der Welt.

feature is the cable railway hovering above the landscape park. The cable railway technology proved to be the most environmentally friendly accessibility option for reaching the Kienberg Park site (56 hectares plus) without any barriers and to connect to the underground station Kienberg Park (Gardens of the World).

The cable railway route runs for 1.5 kilometres, from the Gardens of the World station at Blumberg Dam through to the station on the Kienberg plateau not far from the Wolkenhain and the station Kienberg Park in the southwest part of the area. The journey at a 30 metres height takes a total of five minutes. The cable car can take up to 3,000 guests per hour, who can enjoy the view from a bird's-eye perspective.

The three cable railway stations were designed from one single draft by the architect Kolb Ripke. The buildings, with their green roofs, are part of the landscape, a "green wave" that sweeps from the ground and over the Kienberg.

Wolkenhain
Wolkenhain

Weg zum
Wolkenhain

Path to
Wolkenhain

Wassergärten
Water Gardens

WASSERGÄRTEN

Pantha rei – alles fließt. Diese dem griechischen Philosophen Heraklit zugeschriebene Wendung gilt als Metapher für das Werden und Vergehen. Wasser ist das ureigene Element allen Lebens. Und jeder Gärtner weiß: ohne Wasser kein Wachstum. Auch nicht in der Gartenkunst. Und so bilden die Wassergärten den gartenkünstlerischen Gegenakzent zu dem als Naturraum inszenierten Wuhletal.

Auch in den Gärten der Welt am Kienbergpark spielt das Wasser als Gestaltelement eine wesentliche Rolle. Im traditionellen Chinesischen Garten des wiedergewonnenen Mondes ebenso wie in der Neuinterpretation des chinesischen Gartens als Teil der Internationalen Gartenkabinette, im Orientalischen Garten oder auch im Koreanischen Garten wird die Kraft des Wassers inszeniert. geskes.hack fügen diesem weitläufigen Ensemble die Wassergärten hinzu. Sie schaffen damit Raumbilder, die unter Betonung der vertikalen Elemente insbesondere für verdichtete urbane Räume Raumbeispiele geben, die im Zuge der Anpassungen an den Klimawandel stilbildend wirken.

The meadow slope in the western Kienberg has an event arena, a visitors' centre for the Gardens of the World and Kienberg Park, and a large water playground, but, above all, it has the Water Gardens. Water: before you see it, you hear it. It roars, bubbles and ripples. The water worlds in Kienberg Park are garden galleries in which a diverse range of images of water are atmospherically displayed. The water gardens lie below the belt walk as if lined up on a pearl necklace. This leads through the park meadows to the south at the foot of the Kienberg to the Gardens of the World.

WATER GARDENS

Pantha rei – everything flows. This expression is attributed to the philosopher Heraclitus, and is considered to be a metaphor for the process of becoming and passing. Water is the innate element of all life. And every gardener knows: without water, no growth. This also applies to garden art. Thus, the water gardens

Mit geometrischer Strenge werden in den Wasserwelten einige dieser Traditionen aus der Gartenkunst in moderne Architektursprache gefasst. Ein lichter Baumhain rahmt fünf aufeinanderfolgende Gartenkabinette ein. Eine konzentrierte, zugleich entspannende Atmosphäre umfängt den Besucher in den teils von Hecken, teils von Mauern umschlossenen Gärten. Die gleichmäßig 20 Meter breiten Gartenräume sind geradlinig miteinander verbunden, sodass sich ein weiter Blick bietet. In jedem der Gärten zeigt sich das Wasser in einer anderen Spielart. Vom Blumberger Damm, den Internationalen Gartenkabinetten herkommend, folgt die Choreografie der Gärten in sacht abfallendem Gelände dem Wasserkreislauf von der Quelle bis zur Verdunstung.

Im Quellgarten sind drei verschieden große, kreisrunde Becken in den Boden eingelassen. Sie sind mit dunklem Naturstein ausgekleidet, die Ränder mit rostrotem Cortenstahl eingefasst. In unregelmäßigen Intervallen füllen sich die Quelltöpfe mit Wasser, das nach und nach wieder abfließt. Das Wasser brodelt und sprudelt über dunklen, ungleichmäßig gehauenen Naturstein. Ein lichtes Blätterdach überwölbt knirschenden Kies. Zwischen den Quelltöpfen wandelnd trifft man auf zarte Gräser. Auf steinernen Sitzblöcken lässt es sich wie auf einer Lichtung verweilen, wir können dem abwechslungsreichen Wasserspiel lauschen und zuschauen.

Der Teichgarten besteht aus geometrischen Wasserbecken, die von einem Steg aus Natursteinplatten gequert werden. Auf den ruhigen Wasserflächen spiegeln sich Lotuspflanzen. Eine leise Bewegung des Wassers entsteht lediglich durch den Wind. Die Wasserbecken sind von dunklen Natursteinplatten gefasst, sodass man unmittelbar an das Wasser herantreten und um die Becken herumgehen kann.

Der nächste Gartenraum steigert das Erlebnis des fließenden Wassers zum dramatischen Höhepunkt: Aus waagerechten Rinnen, die in dunkle Natursteinmauern eingelassen sind, stürzen ein großer und zwei kleinere Wasserfälle 5 Meter in die Tiefe. Die massiven Wasserwände bieten ein eindrückliches Spiel zwischen Lichtreflexen, Fließbewegungen und der Geräuschkulisse herabstürzenden Wassers. Auf Trittsteinen in den Wasserbecken kann man sich dem elementaren Erleben des Wassers nähern.

Als Auftakt oder Abschluss gelangt man in den mystisch wirkenden Nebelgarten. Im Kontrast zu den lebendigen Wasserfällen herrscht hier eine ruhige, besinnliche Atmosphäre. Große Felsblöcke markieren den Gartenraum, in dem der Besucher in einen feinen, undurchsichtigen

form a garden art counterpoint to the presentation of the Wuhle Valley as a natural space.

Water as a design element also plays an essential role in the Gardens of the World. The power of water is displayed in both the traditional Chinese Garden of the Reclaimed Moon and the new interpretation of the Chinese Garden that is part of the international garden gallery, in the Oriental Garden and the Korean Garden alike. geskes.hack added these water gardens to the extensive ensemble. This allows them to create spatial settings that, because they emphasise the vertical elements, provide examples of how to use space in condensed urban spaces in particular. These create a new style in the context of adjustments to climate change.

In the water worlds, some of these traditions from garden art are rendered in modern architectural language, with geometric severity. A light grove of trees frames five consecutive garden galleries. A concentrated yet simultaneously relaxed atmosphere envelops the visitor in the gardens, which are partly surrounded by hedges, and partly by walls. The garden areas, uniformly 20 metres wide, are linked together in a straight line, offering a wide view. In each of the gardens, the play of water can be seen in a different way. From the Blumberg Dam, which stems from the International Garden Galleries, the choreography of the gardens follows the water cycle from its source to evaporation, over the gently sloping terrain.

In the spring garden, there are three circular pools of different sizes embedded in the ground. They are lined with dark natural stone and edged with rust-red Corten steel. At irregular intervals, the spring pots fill up with water, which gradually drains off. The water bubbles and gushes over dark, irregularly hewn natural stones. A light leaf canopy arches over scrunching gravel. Strolling between the spring pots, we come to delicate grasses. One can linger awhile, sitting on the stone blocks as if in a clearing, to listen to and watch the varied play of the water.

The pond garden comprises geometric water pools, traversed by a bridge made of natural stone slabs. Lotus plants are reflected in the calm surface of the water. The water is moved only gently by the wind. The water pools are framed by dark natural stone slabs so that you can go directly up to the water and walk around the pools.

The next garden space enhances the experience of the flowing water to create a dramatic highlight:

Nebel eingehüllt wird. Wie in eine Schlucht taucht man zwischen den hohen Wänden ein, die über und über mit einem dichten Pflanzenkleid bedeckt sind. Die Farbigkeit der Pflanzen ist kunstvoll als Bild arrangiert, aus dem Verlauf der unterschiedlichen Grün-, Braun-, Gelb- und Rottöne ergeben sich grafische Muster.

So bildet das Wasser das wesentliche Motiv zwischen Trümmerberg-Kuppe und inszenierten Naturlandschaften entlang des Wuhletals. Ein Volkspark, der in Erweiterung der Gärten der Welt um 20 Hektar mit vielerlei Angeboten aus der globalen Welt der Gartenkultur und der Erlebniswelt vor Ort ein lehrreiches und erlebnisreiches Bild aufwirft, der intensiv und entspannend zugleich wirkt und der ein Statement ist im Sinne der Bedeutung der Fortschreibung der Landschaftspark-Idee in die Zukunft.

from horizontal channels inserted into the dark natural stone walls, one large and two smaller waterfalls flow five metres into the depths. The solid water walls offer an impressive interaction of reflected light, flowing movement, and the background noise of the plummeting water. Stepping stones in the pool allow visitors to approach this elemental water-based experience more closely.

As a prelude or conclusion, one reaches the mist garden, with its mystical appearance. In contrast to the lively waterfalls, it has a calm, reflective atmosphere. Large boulders mark out a garden area, within which the visitor is enveloped in a fine, opaque mist. As with a gorge, one is submerged between high walls, which are completely covered with a dense cloak of plants. The colours of the plants are artfully arranged to create an image, with the various green, brown, yellow, and red tones creating visual patterns.

Thus, water provides a key motif connecting the Trümmerberg summit and the displays of the natural landscapes along the Wuhle Valley. This people's park extends the Gardens of the World by 20 hectares to create an instructive and adventurous picture, offering a diverse sample of the global garden culture and the world of experience on site. It is simultaneously intense and relaxed, and is a statement of the importance of the landscape park idea going forward into the future.

Raumfolgen in den Wassergärten

Room Sequences in the Water Gardens

Quellgarten
Spring Garden

Lotusteich
Lotus Pond

Wasserfälle
Waterfalls

Wassergärten, Raumfolge
Water Gardens, Room Sequence

Nebelgarten
Mist Garden

Nebelgarten
Mist Garden

PARK REICHENBACH / VOGTLAND

Der industrielle Park

The Industrial Estate

Reichenbach, Kleinstadt im Vogtland und Ort der sächsischen Landesgartenschau 2009, hat eine grüne Aue gewonnen: differenziert und detailliert proportioniert, die Hanglagen ebenso wie das Raumbachtal wohltuend akzentuiert und sorgfältig in Szene gesetzt. Dieses Tal prägt die Stadt auf neue Art und Weise.

Reichenbach, a small town in Vogtland and the site of the Saxon Regional Garden Show 2009, has been given a green meadow: nuanced and detailed in proportion, with the slopes as well as the Raumbach valley pleasantly accentuated and meticulously staged. This valley defines the town in a new way.

5. Sächsische Landesgartenschau 2009
Park Reichenbach / Vogtland

Leistungszeitraum: 2006–2009
Leistungsphasen: 1–8
Fläche: 12 Hektar

5. Saxon National Horticultural Show 2009
Park Reichenbach / Vogtland

Construction Period: 2006–2009
Construction Phases: 1–8
Area: 12 hectares

Kletterhügel
Climbing Hill

Raumbachtal
Raumbach Valley

TRANSFORMATION EINES TALS

Am Raumbach nahm die Siedlungsgeschichte, dann die Industriegeschichte Reichenbachs und des gesamten Vogtlandes ihren Ausgang; heute ist aus dem ehemals dicht bebauten und teils ruinösen Industriegebiet die Schauseite der Stadt geworden. Eine radikale Transformation, die selbstbewusst und bruchlos ein neues, farbiges Kapitel für Reichenbach aufschlägt.

Entstanden ist „eine Balance aus überraschenden, neuen Einsichten und sensiblem Umgang mit dem Vorhandenen" (Preisgerichtsurteil zum Landschaftsarchitekturwettbewerb 2005). Es ist besonders dieses gute Auge für die Dimensionen der Landschaft, das die Arbeit von geskes.hack auszeichnet. Einige der gewählten Materialien tragen aufgrund ihres Ortsbezugs dazu bei, dass der neu entstandene Park eine große Selbstverständlichkeit ausstrahlt. Wer Reichenbach kennenlernt, kann sich nicht vorstellen, dass in der Aue nicht immer schon ein Park lag. So wirkt die Arbeit höchst gegenwärtig und selbstverständlich vom ersten Tag an.

TRANSFORMATION OF A VALLEY

The community's history emanated from Raumbach, followed by the industrial history of Reichenbach and the entire Vogtland; today, the formerly heavily built-up and partially ruined industrial zone has become the visible face of the town. This confident, seamless and radical transformation marks a new, colourful chapter for Reichenbach.

What has emerged is a "balance of surprising, new insights and a sensitive handling of existing structures" (in the words of the jury decision from the 2005 landscape architecture competition). It is this eye for the dimensions of the landscape in particular that sets apart the work carried out by geskes.hack. The geographical reference points of some of the chosen materials contribute towards the sense of naturalness radiated by the newly created park. To anyone visiting Reichenbach for the first time, it would appear inconceivable that the meadow didn't always have a park located in it. In

Pink-Pool
Pink Pool

Geschichte fortsetzen, neue Geschichte(n) erfinden: Die Landschaftsarchitekten sprechen nicht zufällig von der Technik des Storytelling, wenn sie ihre Entwurfsarbeit erläutern. Die Landschaftsarchitektur also als narrative Psychologie? Zumindest findet eine intensive Auseinandersetzung mit der Erwartungshaltung der Besucher eines Parks statt. Die Landschaftsarchitekten sind Alltagsbeobachter, und sie wissen zugleich Akzente des Besonderen zu setzen.

Dabei wird der allzu deutliche gestalterische Ruf nach Aufmerksamkeit sorgfältig vermieden. So sind es in Reichenbach eher ein mit wenigen Mitteln in Szene gesetzter Pink Pool – aus einem Abwasserbecken hervorgegangen – oder das mittels Nebeldüsen sinnlich erlebbare ehemalige Becken des Raumbachs, die angesichts der sie umgebenden Zurückhaltung der Parkanlage zu Höhepunkten werden.

WISSEN IMPLIZIT VERMITTELT

Implizites Wissen ist ein gutes Stichwort für die Arbeiten von geskes.hack, die wenig behaupten und doch so viel vermitteln.

Der Spaß am Entdecken der Geschichte und der Geschichten eines Ortes ist dem sogenannten Park der Generationen in Reichenbach anzusehen. Einzelne Aspekte dieser Geschichte werden aufgegriffen und in der Gestaltung des Parks weitererzählt. In Reichenbach ist es gerade kein pädagogisch aufbereitetes, nach außen getragenes Wissen um die Geschichte eines Ortes, das die Landschaftsarchitektur prägt. Die Industriegeschichte der Reichenbacher Aue, die durch die Textilindustrie geprägt war, ist im Park thematisch und auch gestalterisch mehrfach präsent, ohne jedoch eine vermeintliche Geschichte zu rekonstruieren. Stattdessen ist das Farbmuster des zentralen Festplatzes eine Reminiszenz an historische Webmuster.

Der einst zur Abwasserrinne verkommene Raumbach wurde innerhalb des Tals umgelegt, ein Relikt des ehemaligen, mit Ziegeln aufgemauerten Kanalbettes blieb jedoch bestehen. Durch dieses Bett kann man nun inmitten von feuchtigkeitsliebenden Pflanzen spazieren. Feiner Nebel unterstreicht die Unwirklichkeit der Situation und lässt den einen oder anderen Besucher in die Erinnerung an das dicht bebaute Raumbachtal fallen. Im Fabrikgarten Schreiterer wird mit Färberpflanzen in der Art der Floristik gearbeitet.

So ist der Park eine vielfache Metapher für den Wandel Reichenbachs. Wie mehrere sächsische Städte war Reichenbach von der Textilindustrie und dem Maschinenbau

this respect, the work has appeared highly contemporary and natural from the very first day. Continuing the story, making up new stories: it is no coincidence that the landscape architects talk about storytelling techniques when explaining their design work. So, is this landscape architecture as narrative psychology? At the very least, it involves an intensive discussion regarding the expectations of the visitors to a park. The landscape architects are observers of the everyday. At the same time they know how to emphasise special features.

In doing so, they carefully avoid calling attention to their creativity in too obvious a manner. In Reichenbach, it is shown by a Pink Pool, a scene created with the minimum of elements from a pool of waste water, and by the former Raumbach pool that is turned into a sensory perception experience by nozzle jets that become highlights within the subdued surroundings of the park complex.

CONVEYING KNOWLEDGE IMPLICITLY

Implicit knowledge is a good keyword for the work produced by geskes.hack Landscape Architects, which claims so little and yet conveys so much.

The joy of discovering the history and the stories of a place can be observed in the Park of Generations in Reichenbach. Individual aspects of this history are taken up and retold in the design of the park. In Reichenbach, it is not any particular academic knowledge about the history of a place projected onto the landscape that defines the landscape architecture. The industrial history of the Reichenbach meadow (characterised by the textile industry) is represented in many ways in the park both thematically and creatively, but without reconstructing an alleged history. Instead, the colour pattern of the central festival site is reminiscent of historical weaving patterns.

The Raumbach, which at one time deteriorated into a wastewater channel, was relocated within the valley. However, a relic of the former canal bed remained, built up with bricks. It is now possible to take a walk through this waterway bed, surrounded by plants that thrive on moisture. The fine mist underlines the unreality of the situation, and may put a visitor in mind of the heavily built up Raumbach valley. In the Schreiterer factory garden, plants used in dyeing are arranged in the manner of floriculture.

Festplatz
Festival Site

Färbergarten
Dyer's Garden

Farbräume
Colour Spaces

Salbeiwellen
Sage Waves

geprägt; nach deren Ende musste die Stadt ihre Zukunft neu definieren. Der zur Gartenschau 2009 entstandene Park der Generationen ist eines der Instrumente auf diesem Weg. Und so total wie der Bruch mit der Industriegeschichte ist auch die Veränderung ausgefallen.

FARBEN ZEICHNEN RÄUME

Das dunkle Grün des Waldhanges im Süden der Stadt Reichenbach und der Raumbachaue wechselt mit dem helleren Grün von gezielt gesetzten Säulenbuchen. Über die Aue schweift der Blick in ein sanftes, teils auch sattes, immer leuchtendes Grün einer Parkwiese, die durch Frühjahrsblüher, durch farbenfrohe Staudenpflanzungen, durch Rosenbeete und einige Buschgruppen gesprenkelt ist. Den Hang hin zur Stadt markieren Wärme und Sonne liebende, also blütenreiche Pflanzen. Die Stadtsilhouette, farblich in Beige bis Ockergelb gehalten, teils mit roten Dachziegeln, teils mit dunklen Schieferdächern gedeckt, tritt vor allem durch die Kirche St. Peter und Paul hervor. Der Waldhang findet in der Stadtkulisse ein starkes Gegenüber, die Parkwiese vermittelt zwischen beiden.

Es ist eine Qualität des mittels Farbe Geschaffenen, dass hier nicht etwas bunt angemalt wurde, um eine Fröhlichkeit zu signalisieren, sondern dass es gelungen ist, die eher sanften Farben zum Thema dieser Stadt der Textilindustrie zu machen.

In this respect, the park is a multiple metaphor for the changes in Reichenbach. Like many Saxon cities, Reichenbach was characterised by the textile industry and mechanical engineering; when this came to an end, the town had to redefine its future. The Park of Generations created for the Garden Show 2009 is one of the tools for moving down this path. Despite a complete break with the town's industrial history, there has been no corresponding change.

COLOURS DRAW SPACES

The dark green of the forest slope to the south of the town of Reichenbach and the Raumbach meadow alternates with the lighter green of positioned column beeches. One's gaze passes over the river meadowland to the gentle sometimes lush and always lustrous green of a park meadow dotted with spring flowers, colourful shrub plantations, rose beds, and some groups of bushes. The slope facing the town is marked by heat and sun-loving, richly blossoming plants. The town silhouette is beige to ochre yellow in colour and features a mixture of red roof tiles and dark slate roofs, with the church of St. Peter and St. Paul as a distinctive feature. The forest slope finds a strong counterpart in the townscape, whilst the park meadow mediates between both.

Skateanlage
Skate Park

Stadtterrasse
City Terrace

DER BALANCIERTE TALRAUM

Das neue Raumbachtal ist kein Rückgriff auf vorindustrielle Zeiten. Dazu trägt vor allem die Waldbühne bei. Dieser Kulturort kontrastiert den Eindruck einer tiefgrünen Waldwildnis gegenüber der Stadt. Halbrunde Sitzstufen in Beton, asymmetrisch verteilt und durch weitere Bäume akzentuiert, laden zum Kulturgenuss an den Rand des Waldes. Und zugleich zu einem sehr schönen Blick auf die Stadt Reichenbach.

Besonders diese Idee der Waldbühne, platziert in den Saum des Waldhanges hinein, schafft als Gegenüber zur Stadt wiederum eine bauliche, eine kulturelle Nutzung, was erheblich zum Eindruck eines gut ausbalancierten Raumes beiträgt.

Raumbezüge wurden nicht nur im Bereich der Raumbachaue geschaffen. Sehr überzeugend ist auch der Blick von der Skateanlage im Bereich des ehemaligen Güterbahnhofs der Stadt durch die Baumkronen des neu angepflanzten Arboretums hindurch auf die Stadtkirche. Mit den

Waldbühne
Forest Stage

One quality of this colour creation is that nothing was painted in colour here in order to signal gaiety. Instead, it succeeds in using rather soft colours as a theme for this textile industry city.

THE BALANCED SPACE OF THE VALLEY

The new Raumbach valley is not a throwback to pre-industrial times. In particular, the forest stage contributes towards this. This cultural site contrasts the atmosphere of a deep green forest wilderness with the town. The concrete semicircular stepped seating, asymmetrically distributed and accentuated by additional trees, invites visitors to enjoy culture at the edge of the forest. At the same time, they can take in a very beautiful view over the town of Reichenbach.

In particular, the idea of the forest stage, positioned on the edge of the forest slope, appears as a

Waldbühne
Forest Stage

Parkeingang
Park Entrance

Mitteln der Landschaftsarchitektur werden die Raumbezüge erkennbar.

Fast beiläufig und erst auf den zweiten Blick auffallend sind dagegen die großen Steinblöcke aus Theumaer Fruchtschiefer, die aufgrund ihrer Proportionen wie selbstverständlich als Sitzgelegenheiten fungieren. Theumaer Fruchtschiefer wurde aufgrund des regionalen Bezuges gewählt, dieses Gestein steht in der Nähe an und wurde auch in der Baugeschichte des Ortes vielfach verarbeitet. geskes.hack Landschaftsarchitekten nutzen diese Schieferblöcke grob behauen, jeder einzelne wurde individuell im Steinbruch ausgewählt. Das Material bietet eine Anknüpfung zur Identität des Ortes. In vielen weiteren Parks von geskes.hack wird dieser Schiefer seit der Arbeit für Reichenbach ebenfalls verwendet.

Trotz ihrer individuellen Stärken ist keines dieser Elemente allein prägend für den gesamten Park. Materialen und Elemente werden immer in Kontrastierungen eingesetzt, und dennoch vermitteln sie zwischen den Atmosphären. So ist der farbig gestrichene Beton zugleich eine farbliche Reminiszenz an die Laubfarben der Bäume des Arboretums ebenso wie eine förmliche Bezugnahme auf den benachbarten Skateparcours.

ORTE UND AKZENTE

Ähnlich beziehungsreich neu interpretiert wird das Umfeld des traditionsreichen Ziegelbaus des ehemaligen Reichenbacher Wasserwerks am Fuße des Waldhangs. Dieses Gebäude blieb als eines der wenigen aus der Industriegeschichte des Ortes erhalten. Von Grund auf saniert, beherbergt der Bau heute Ausstellungsräume.

Im Park wird auf das ehemalige Wasserwerk unmittelbar Bezug genommen. Den Spielplatz des Parks legten die Landschaftsarchitekten an diesen besonderen Ort. Auf die spielerische Aneignung der Landschaft legen geskes.hack besonderen Wert. Und so ist das gesamte Spielangebot auf das Fließen des Wassers ins Tal ausgerichtet. In einer Verbindung von Eigenkreationen und vorgefertigten Spielelementen ist ein Spielplatz entstanden, der dem Ort entspricht, ein Thema besetzt und zugleich einen hohen Spielwert aufgrund einer großen Vielzahl an spielerischen Möglichkeiten des Stauens, des Umleitens, des Pumpens und des Spritzens von Wasser aufweist. Dieser Wasserspielplatz wird von allen Altersgruppen sehr gut angenommen, und da sich die Spielenden gegenseitig sehr stark beeinflussen, indem sie Wasser stauen oder fließen lassen, entsteht eine eifrige Kommunikation untereinander.

contrast to the town, creating a structural, cultural functional area that makes a considerable contribution to the impression of a well-balanced space.

These spatial references go beyond the Raumbach meadow. The view of the skate park in the vicinity of the town's former goods depot is also very impressive; through the tree crowns of the newly planted arboretum to the town church. The tools of landscape architecture make the spatial references recognisable.

By contrast, the large stone blocks made of Theuma slate, ideally proportioned to serve as seating, are almost casually conspicuous, only striking the viewer at a second glance. The Theuma slate was chosen for the regional reference: this stone is from close by and was often used in the community's construction history. geskes.hack Landscape Architects use roughly trimmed slate blocks, each one individually chosen in the quarry. The material offers a link to the identity of the place. Since the work at Reichenbach was completed, this slate has likewise been used in many other parks by geskes.hack.

In spite of their individual strengths, none of these elements alone characterises the entire park. The materials and elements are always used with contrast in mind, and yet they mediate between the atmospheres. In this respect, the colourfully painted concrete is at the same time a colourful echo of the foliage colours of the trees in the arboretum. Simultaneously, its form references the neighbouring skate course.

PLACES AND HIGHLIGHTS

The environs of the traditional brick building of the former Reichenbach waterworks at the forest slope's foot are similarly rich in reinterpreted connections. This building is one of the few that survive from the location's industrial history. Renovated from the ground up, the building today accommodates exhibition rooms.

In the park, direct reference is made to the former water works. The landscape architects placed the park playground in this special place. geskes.hack attach great importance to the playful appropriation of the landscape. Thus, everything presented here is orientated on the flowing of the water into the valley. Connecting their own creations with prefabricated play elements creates a playground that suits the place, addresses a topic, and at the same time demonstrates high play value, with plenty of play options that

Holzdecks
am Raumbach

Wooden Decks
at Raumbach

Das verwendete Material dieses Spielplatzes beschränkt sich auf hölzerne Rinnen, sogenannte Kandeln, und Pumpen sowie Schleusen aus Edelstahl. In Kinderhöhe montiert und mit Kies unterbaut führen mehrere dieser Rinnen die Wasserströme zu einem Sandspielbereich im Tal, der sich sehr gut als Matschspielplatz eignet.

Der Gesamteindruck überzeugt auch deshalb, weil der Spielplatz in die Hanglandschaft eingebunden ist. Sitz- und Lagerangebote aus Schieferblöcken für Kinder wie für Eltern sind beidseitig am Rande der Kandeln in den Hang platziert, vorhandener Baum- und Strauchbewuchs wurde integriert und bietet ein angenehmes Wechselspiel aus Sonnen- und Schattenplätzen. Die Zurückhaltung in der Materialverwendung lässt diesen Spielplatz dann sichtbar hervortreten, wenn er intensiv genutzt wird, ansonsten aber nicht aus dem Gesamtbild des Talraumes herausfallen.

Es ist diese Mehrfachbindung, die keine der gestalterischen Ideen unvermittelt im Raum stehen lässt. Statt einfacher Kontrastierungen werden immer Verbindungen und Gegensätze im Material, den Farben und Formen und auch den Funktionen angeboten. So wird aus einem stimmigen Park zugleich ein spannender Raum – eine Raumerzählung.

astonish and divert featuring the pumping and spraying of water. This water playground is very well received by all age groups, and, since those playing have a great influence on each other by impeding the water or letting it flow, eager communication between them occurs.

The material used in this playground is limited to wooden channels, so-called gutters, and pumps, plus sluices made of stainless steel. Assembled at a child's height and with gravel below, several of these channels lead the flows of water to a sand play area in the valley that makes an ideal mud playground.

The overall atmosphere is also effective because the playground is integrated into the slope landscape. Seating and camping sites made of slate blocks for both children and parents are placed on both sides of the gutters in the slope; the existing trees and shrubs were integrated, creating a pleasant interaction of sun and shade areas. The restrained use of material makes this playground visible when it is in intensive use. Otherwise, however, it blends into the overall view of the valley.

It is this multiple bond that ensures that none of the creative ideas are left in isolation. Instead of simple contrasts, the materials, the colours and forms, and the functions always offer connections and oppositions. Thus, a harmonious park simultaneously becomes an exciting space. This is a spatial narrative.

Wasserspielplatz mit Kandeln

Water Playground with Gutters

NATURGARTEN SCHWERIN

Vulkane im Naturgarten
Volcanoes in a Nature Garden

Der Park als Spielraum gewinnt als analoges Pendant zur virtuellen Welt des Digitalen an Bedeutung. Bewegungen kann man nicht nur mit dem Daumen am Joystick trainieren, und die Spielenden, vor allem die Jugendlichen, wissen dies. Sie probieren sich und ihre Beziehungen zur Schwerkraft, zur Hebelwirkung, zur Schnellkraft an allerlei Gelegenheiten aus und gestalten sich so ihren eigenen Erfahrungsraum. Die Landschaftsarchitektur muss umso mehr beeindrucken, muss Herausforderungen und Attraktionen schaffen, um das Interesse der suchenden Jugendclique zu wecken.

The park as a play area is gaining in importance as an analogous counterpoint to virtual digital worlds. Exercising merely by using a thumb to move the joystick isn't exercising, and those playing, particularly the young people, know this. Thus, they like to test themselves at every opportunity: in relation to gravity, to leverage, to high-speed strength. They create their own experience spheres. This means that landscape architecture has to work all the harder to impress, to create challenges and attractions, and to arouse the interest of this questing youth cohort.

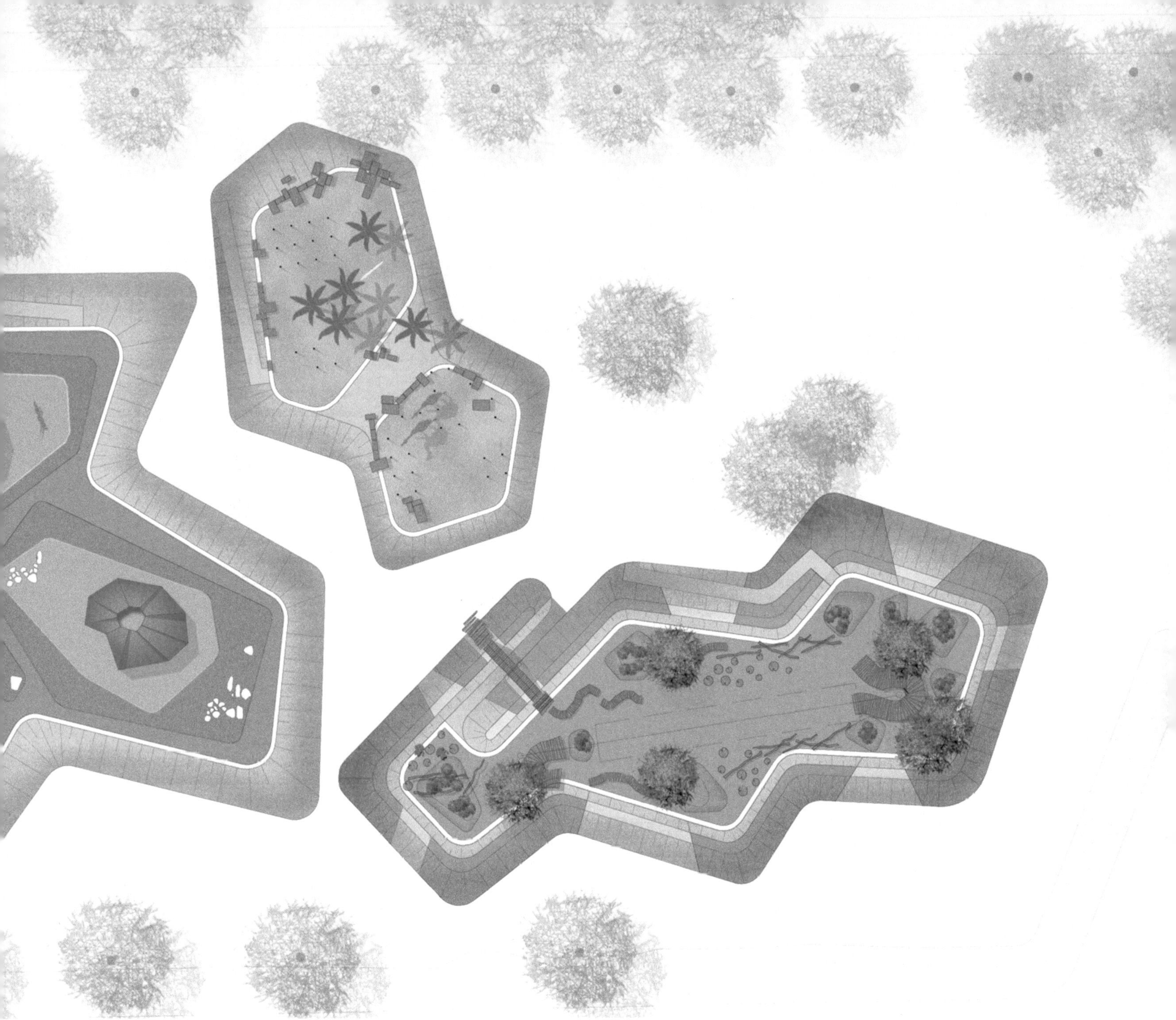

Bundesgartenschau Schwerin 2009
Naturgarten

Leistungszeitraum: 2006–2009
Leistungsphasen: 1–8
Fläche: 7 Hektar

Federal Garden Show Schwerin 2009
Nature Garden

Construction Period: 2006–2009
Construction Phases: 1–8
Area: 7 hectares

Wüstenland
Desert Wasteland

Steppenland
Steppe Landscape

SPIELERLEBNIS

Das pädagogische vorgeplante Spielerlebnis kann mit der Erlebniserwartung nicht mehr mithalten. Daher sind viele Spielangebote, die geskes.hack erdenken, nicht von der Stange oder aus dem Katalog zu haben. Sie entstehen individuell auf den Ort bezogen und zeigen oftmals das Unerwartete.

Schwerin, beschauliche Landeshauptstadt Mecklenburg-Vorpommerns, hat mit der Bundesgartenschau 2009 die Geschichte der Gartenkunst für ein großes Publikum wiederentdeckt. Insoweit wurden die Erwartungen und Interessen des traditionellen Gartenschau-Publikums hervorragend bedient. Zugleich hat der „Spielplatz der Atolle" im Bereich Naturgarten am Schweriner See ein völlig unerwartetes, auf den ersten Blick sogar befremdliches Zeichen gesetzt – und so die Stadt um einen der attraktivsten Spielplätze bereichert, die in den letzten Jahren gebaut wurden. Mit den Regionen Feuerland, Wüstenland und vor allem mit dem Sumpfland bezieht sich der Spielplatz der Atolle auf die vorgefundene Lage im Raum am Ufer des Schweriner Sees unter

PLAY EXPERIENCE

Educational pre-planned play experiences can no longer keep pace with expectations of experience. Therefore, many of the play facilities that geskes.hack devise are not off the peg or from a catalogue. They are created individually, tailored to the location, and they frequently show us something unexpected.

Schwerin, the tranquil state capital of Mecklenburg-West Pomerania, rediscovered the history of garden art for a wide audience with its Federal Garden Show 2009. In this respect, the expectations and interests of the traditional garden show audience were met exceptionally well. At the same time, the "Playground of the Atolls" in Schwerin Lake's nature garden area took a completely unexpected, and at first glance even disconcerting, stance – but in this way it enriched the city by giving it one of the most attractive playgrounds built in recent years. With the region's land of fire, desert wasteland and above all the marshland, the

Vulkanland
Volcanic Landscape

Flößerstangen in der Auenwiese
Raftsman Rods in the Meadow

Holzsteg im Auenwald

Wooden Bridge in the Floodplain Forest

dichten Baumkronen. Der Spielplatz spinnt diese Lage aber zugleich weiter, indem das Sumpfland als Spielmotiv durch Wüste und Feuerland erweitert wird. Die Spielenden können dort quasi die ganze Welt als Welt der Kontraste entdecken. Ein traditionelles Motiv der Gartenkunst, umgesetzt in Form eines Spielplatzes.

NATUR CONTRA GARTEN?

Generell löste die Frage nach dem Verhältnis zwischen Natur und Garten bereits in der Vorbereitung auf die Gartenschau in Schwerin erhebliche Diskussionen aus: Stört, zerstört Garten(schau) gar die Natur? Durch die parkkulturelle Intervention eines Spielplatzes als Naturerlebnis haben geskes.hack Landschaftsarchitekten eine ganz eigene, bildwirksame Antwort auf diese Grundsatzfrage gegeben.

Schon von Weitem schimmert das Farbspiel aus Rot und Orange durch die Bäume und Büsche hindurch; so lockt der Spielplatz Jung und Alt magisch an. Farbig gestrichene, halbierte Holzstämme weisen den unsicheren Weg. Betritt

Holzstämme in Orchideenwiese

Wooden Trunks in the Orchid Meadow

Playground of the Atolls references the existing situation on the banks of Lake Schwerin, below the dense treetops. However, at the same time the playground continues on with this situation in which the marshland is extended as a play motif through the desert and the land of fire. Here, those at play can virtually discover a whole world, a world of contrasts. A traditional garden art motif is turned into a playground.

NATURE VERSUS GARDEN?

In general the question of the relationship between nature and the garden had already prompted considerable discussion during preparations for the garden show in Schwerin: does a garden show actualy disturb and destroy nature? Through the cultural park intervention of a natural experience playground, geskes.hack Landscape Architects have offered their very own, effective answer to this basic question.

man den Spielplatz der Atolle, sind es vor allem die Vulkane, die neugierig machen. Ein neuer, auch fremdartiger Akzent an diesem naturnah belassenen Uferabschnitt des Schweriner Sees, der aber – genau platziert – im Raumprogramm der Garten-Schau der „Sieben Gärten" seine Legitimation findet und als siebter Garten die Entdeckungsreise der Gartenkunst entlang des Schweriner Sees entscheidend bereichert.

SPIELPLATZ DER ATOLLE

Der Spielplatz der Atolle im Park am Schweriner See – gegenüber des Schweriner Schlosses – ist weit mehr als ein eigenständiger Beitrag für Kinder. Als ein Ort der aktiven, spielerischen Aneignung von Raum gelingt es ihm, den ansonsten auf Flanieren und Gartengenuss ausgerichteten Besuch Schwerins aufzuwerten. Aufgrund der Arbeit von geskes.hack Landschaftsarchitekten in Entwurf und Umsetzung ist dieses Angebot kein Fremdkörper, sondern Anreicherung innerhalb einer weitgehend den historischen Vorbildern folgenden, diese rekonstruierenden Gartenlandschaft.

Die Atolle sind Teil der „Sieben Gärten" Schwerins und zugleich so eigenständig komponiert, dass dieser Ort die Geschichte der Weltläufigkeit und des Entdeckertums, für die Gartenkunstgeschichte ja auch steht, einmal aus einer ganz anderen Perspektive, der des Abenteuers, erzählt. Die Erzählung ist ebenso spannend wie in sich schlüssig aufgebaut; ein mutiges Experiment inmitten historischer Gartenlandschaft, ein farbenfroher Akzent im grünen Schwerin – und das wohl zweitwichtigste Bildmotiv nach dem Schweriner Schloss am See.

Even from a distance, the interplay of colour between red and orange shimmers through the trees and bushes; this is how the playground magically entices young and old alike. Colourfully painted halved wooden trunks mark out the precarious path. As one enters the Playground of the Atolls, it is the volcanoes in particular that arouse curiosity. This emphasis on the natural section of the shore of Lake Schwerin may be new and even unfamiliar, but it is legitimated by its careful placing within the spatial programme of the "Seven Gardens" garden show. As the seventh garden, it decisively enriches the voyage of discovery along Lake Schwerin.

PLAYGROUND OF THE ATOLLS

The Playground of the Atolls in the park on Lake Schwerin – opposite Schwerin Castle – is far more than an independent contribution for children. As a place where space is actively and playfully appropriated, it succeeds in enhancing a visit otherwise geared to strolling and enjoying the garden. Due to the work created by geskes.hack Landscape Architects in its design and implementation, this offering is not a foreign body but an enriching feature within this reconstructed garden landscape that largely follows historical role models.

The Atolls are part of the "Seven Gardens" of Schwerin. At the same time, they have been composed so that this location once again tells the story of the worldliness and the joys of discovery (and, after all, this is an important aspect of garden art), from a completely different perspective: that of adventure. This tale is exciting as well as being logically grounded. It is a brave experiment in the middle of a historical garden landscape, a colourful highlight set amid green Schwerin. And undoubtedly the second most important image motif after Schwerin Castle on the Lake.

Spiel-Vulkan
Toy Volcano

Spielplatz der Atolle
Playground of the Atolls

Im Inneren eines Spiel-Vulkans

Inside a Toy Volcano

FISCHHOFPARK TIRSCHENREUTH

Inselstadt mit Fischkästen
Island Town with Fish Boxes

„Das Tuchmacherstädtchen Tirschenreuth liegt gar schön." Johann Wolfgang von Goethe war wohl auf dem Weg nach Italien, als er 1786 Tirschenreuth in der Oberpfalz besuchte. Wie auch andere Orte ist Tirschenreuth stolz auf ein solches Goethe-Zitat. Goethe war auf seinem Weg nach Italien erwartungsvoll, bereit, das Schöne zu sehen – und Schönes auf dem Wege in sein Reisetagebuch zu notieren. Und darin liegt das Geheimnis, das geskes.hack Landschaftsarchitekten angewendet haben bei ihrer Gestaltung des Fischhofparks in Tirschenreuth: das Schöne auf dem Weg sehen wollen!

"The cloth-making town of Tirschenreuth lies in a beautiful location." Johann Wolfgang von Goethe was on his way to Italy when he visited Tirschenreuth in Upper Palatinate in 1786. Like many other places, Tischenreuth is proud of this citation. Goethe was travelling to Italy, full of anticipation, ready to see the country's beauty – and to write about it in his travel diary on the way. And therein lies the secret behind the geskes.hack Landscape Architects' design for the Fischhof Park in Tirschenreuth: wanting to see the beauty on the way!

Natur in Tirschenreuth 2013
Fischhofpark

Leistungszeitraum: 2009–2013
Leistungsphasen: 1–9
Fläche: 20 Hektar

Nature in Tirschenreuth 2013
Fischhof Park

Construction Period: 2009–2013
Construction Phases: 1–9
Area: 20 hectares

Fischhofbrücke mit neuem Stadtteich

Fischhof Bridge with New City Pond

Oberer Stadtteich
Upper City Pond

GAR SCHÖN GELEGEN

Kein Ort ist per se schön – Orte wie Menschen werden als schön *angesehen*. Die Schönheit liegt im Auge des Betrachters. Diese dem schottischen Philosophen und Universalgelehrten David Hume zugeschriebene Erkenntnis, die Immanuel Kant zu seiner *Kritik der Urteilskraft* und zu seiner Lehre vom „ästhetischen Urteil" inspirierte, stellte am Vorabend der Aufklärung den Menschen in den Mittelpunkt des Denkens. In der Kunst der Renaissance wird der Betrachter, der selbstbewusste Mensch, erstmals selbst zum Thema.

Tirschenreuth war zur damaligen Zeit Teil des Klosters Waldsassen und hatte von diesem schon 1364 die Stadtrechte verliehen bekommen. Der Renaissance-Erker des Tirschenreuther Rathauses erinnert an diese Jahrhunderte. Die Teichwirtschaft in Tirschenreuth, dem Zentrum des „Stiftlandes" in der heutigen Oberpfalz (Bayern), war damals die wirtschaftliche Grundlage. Später wurde Tirschenreuth

WELL SITUATED

No place is beautiful in itself – places, like people, are *seen* as beautiful. Beauty lies in the eyes of the beholder. This realisation, attributed to the Scottish philosopher and scholar David Hume, who inspired Immanuel Kant to write his *Critique of Judgement* and to create his doctrine of "aesthetic judgement", was articulated on the eve of the Enlightenment, and placed the human being at the centre of thought. In Renaissance art, the beholder becomes the self-confident man. For the first time, the beholder is the subject of the art.

At that time Tirschenreuth was part of the Waldsassen Monastery. It was awarded city rights in 1364. The Renaissance bay window of the Tirschenreuth town hall recalls these centuries. At the time, the economy of Tirschenreuth, the centre of the "Stiftland" in present day Upper Palatinate (Bavaria), was based

als Tuchmacherstadt und dann aufgrund der Porzellanherstellung bekannt.

Neu interpretierte „Fischkästen" lenken heute die Blicke; und das bedeutsame Ensemble aus Fischhof, steinerner Brücke und den umgebenden Stadtteichen ist im Zuge der Parkgestaltung wieder sichtbar geworden. Dieses Ensemble, das Tirschenreuth, Teichpfanne und Klosterwirtschaft quasi auf einen Blick erklärt, war zwischenzeitlich an den Stadtrand gerückt worden und nicht gut angesehen. Mit der Wiederherstellung der Blicke und Blickpunkte, dem historisch einmaligen Ensemble, wird Tirschenreuth dem „gar schön" heute wieder gerecht.

TEICHE, TAUSENDE TEICHE

Tausende Teiche mit einer Wasserfläche von etwa 2000 Hektar prägen den Landkreis Tirschenreuth. Hieran galt es in der Parkgestaltung der Gegenwart anzuknüpfen.

1217, als die Ortschaft an das Kloster Waldsassen fiel, begann in Tirschenreuth die intensive Fischzucht. Zisterziensermönche bestellten einen Fischermeister, der die Stadtteiche sachkundig bewirtschaftete. Mit der Aufhebung und Enteignung des Klosters Waldsassen im Zuge der Säkularisierung im Jahre 1803 war eine ordnungsgemäße Bewirtschaftung der Stadtteiche nicht mehr gegeben. So wurden die beiden Tirschenreuther Stadtteiche 1807/08 trockengelegt, um Nutzflächen für Ackerbau und Viehzucht zu erhalten.

Mit dem Trockenfallen der Teiche verlor die Stadt eine städtebauliche Einmaligkeit: die Rahmung der Stadt durch den *Oberen* und *Unteren Stadtteich*. Die 1748–1750 von Frater Philipp Muttone nach dem Vorbild einer steinernen Brücke in Regensburg erbaute repräsentative Fischhofbrücke erinnerte zwei Jahrhunderte lang als Rellkt – frei auf einer Wiese stehend – an die einst blühende Fischzucht in Tirschenreuth.

STADT UND WASSER

Mehr als 100 Jahre war die Stadt Tirschenreuth bestrebt, die beiden einst prägenden Stadtteiche und damit das historische Stadtbild wiederherzustellen. Mit der Ausrichtung der Gartenschau „Natur in der Stadt" im Jahr 2013 konnte dieses Anliegen umgesetzt werden. Die auf einer Wiese stehende Fischhofbrücke überspannt heute wieder eine Wasserfläche. Durch die Arbeit von geskes.hack Landschaftsarchitekten wurde die Topografie der prägenden Stadträume Altstadtkuppe, Talraum und Klosterinsel herausgearbeitet.

on fish farming. Later Tirschenreuth became known as a weaver town, and later again for porcelain manufacture.

Newly interpreted "fish boxes" catch the eye today. The park design has made the significant ensemble comprising the Fischhof, the stone bridge, and the surrounding city ponds visible again in the course of the park design. This ensemble, which explains Tirschenreuth, the pond area and the monastery economy practically at a glance, had been shifted to the edge of the city, where it did not appear to advantage. With the restoration of the views and viewpoints and the historically unique ensemble, Tirschenreuth is once again "well situated".

PONDS, THOUSANDS OF PONDS

Thousands of ponds with a water surface of around 2,000 hectares characterise the district of Tirschenreuth. The idea was to connect with the park design of the present.

In 1217, when the location became the property of the Waldsassen Monastery, intensive fish farming began in Tirschenreuth. Cistercian monks appointed a fishing master who competently managed the city ponds. The dissolution and dispossession of Waldsassen Monastery during the secularisation of 1803, meant that proper management of the city ponds was no longer guaranteed. Thus both of the Tirschenreuth urban ponds were drained in 1807/08 in order to acquire effective space for arable farming and cattle breeding.

With the ponds becoming dry, the city lost its unique urban feature of framing of the city by the *upper* and *lower* city pond. The prestigious Fischhof bridge, built in 1748–1750 by Frater Philipp Muttone based on an example of a stone bridge in Regensburg – freely standing in a meadow – is a two-hundred-year old relic of the once booming fish farming industry in Tirschenreuth.

CITY AND WATER

For over a hundred years, the city of Tirschenreuth endeavoured to restore both the once characteristic city ponds and the historic cityscape. It finally became possible to implement this during organisation of the garden show "Nature in the city" in 2013. The Fischhof Bridge

Fischkästen
Fish Boxes

Oberer Stadtteich mit Fischkasten

Upper City Pond with Fish Boxes

Die Teichanlage um die Fischhofinsel konnte teilweise nach historischem Vorbild wiederhergestellt werden. Mit dem Fischhofpark ist es gelungen, zu einer Steigerung der Attraktivität der gesamten Stadt beizutragen, indem die Stadt mit dem neu geschaffenen Seepark verbunden wurde. Die zurückgewonnene Teichlandschaft ist für die Naherholung und für den Naturschutz von Bedeutung und ebenso eine Bereicherung für den aufstrebenden Tourismus in der Region.

Den Landschaftsarchitekten gelang es, rund um den Stadtteich einen qualitativ hochwertigen Grün- und Erholungsbereich zu schaffen. Die „durchgängige intensive und sensible Bearbeitung aller städtebaulich relevanten Teilbereiche" war ausschlaggebend dafür, dass die Jury diese Arbeit im Wettbewerb um die Gestaltung der Gartenschau 2013 mit dem ersten Preis bedachte. „Der Entwurf geht sehr sensibel auf die örtlichen Besonderheiten ein. Die Gestaltung wirkt spannungsreich und dabei gleichzeitig selbstverständlich." Heute ist der Fischhofpark das touristische Merkzeichen der Stadt Tirschenreuth.

Es ist dieser behutsame und zugleich offensive Umgang mit der Historie des Ortes, der den Fischhofpark auszeichnet. Im Entwurf wurde die Bedeutung historischer Identitäten klar sichtbar, indem neue, zeitgenössische Identitäten hinzugefügt wurden. Die Landschaftsarchitektur ermöglicht hier quasi die Renovierung einer sehr alten, zwei Jahrhunderte lang überformten Identität. Und dennoch entwickelten geskes.hack keine Rekonstruktion der Vergangenheit, sondern einen zeitgemäßen Entwurf für Tirschenreuth. Die Neugestaltung und Aufwertung der Stadtkante verknüpft den Park mit der Altstadt, mit dem attraktiven und vitalen Kern der Stadt, dem Ensemble aus lang gestrecktem Stadtplatz, altem Rathaus mit Renaissance-Erker und flankierenden Bürgerhäusern.

Durch die Freiräumung des Geländes der Schels-Brauerei entstand der durch zwei neue Baukörper gefasste Platz am See – und mit diesem Platz die wichtigste Verbindung zwischen Innenstadt und neuem Stadtpark. Wie ein Fenster öffnet der Platz neue Perspektiven aus der dicht bebauten Altstadt in die Landschaft und auf den Fischhof. Diese städtebauliche Stärkung wird betont durch eine neue Brücke hinüber zum Fischhof. Die Brücke bildet eine Landmarke und ist ein funktionales Schlüsselelement des neuen Stadterlebens. Denn diese neue Brücke ermöglicht die Blicke auf die Stadt und den Landschaftsraum in einem Rundgang.

Die Landschaftsarchitekten unterstrichen ihre große städtebauliche Geste einer neuen Verbindung zwischen

that once stood in a meadow today spans a water surface once again. The work of geskes.hack Landscape Architects has revealed the topography of the characteristic urban space: the old town crest, the valley area, and the monastery island.

It was possible to restore the pond area around Fischhof Island partly based on historical models. The Fischhof Park succeeded in contributing towards an increase in the appeal of the entire city by linking the city to the newly created lake park. The recaptured pond landscape is significant for local recreation and for nature conservation. It also benefits the up-and-coming tourism industry in the region.

The landscape architects succeeded in creating a high-quality green space and recreation area around the city pond. The "consistently intensive and sensitive processing of all relevant urban sub areas" was a critical factor in the jury awarding first prize for this work in the garden show design competition 2013. "The design deals very sensitively with the local conditions. The design appears exciting and thereby at the same time natural." Today, Fischhof Park is the tourist landmark for the city of Tirschenreuth.

It is this cautious and simultaneously challenging way of dealing with the history of the location that sets Fischhof Park apart. In the design, the significance of historical identities was made visible through the addition of new, contemporary identities. This is a case of landscape architecture practically enabling the renovation of a very old identity reshaped over two centuries. geskes.hack, however, did not reconstruct the past. Instead, they created a contemporary design for Tirschenreuth. The new design and enhancement of the city periphery link the park with the old town: the attractive and vital centre of the city, with its ensemble of the elongated city square, old town hall with its Renaissance bay windows and flanking community centres.

The clearing of the Schels Brewery site allowed the Place at the Sea to be created within a frame of two new structures – with this location as the most important connection between the town centre and the new city park. Like a window, this place opens up new perspectives: from the densely built-up old town into the landscape and the Fischhof. This urban reinforcement is emphasised by a new bridge connecting to the Fischhof. The bridge forms a landmark and is a functional key element in the new city experience. This is

Historische Fischhofbrücke und Überlaufwehr

Ancient Fischhof Bridge and Overflow Weir

Altstadt und Fischhofinsel durch eine Materialfolge, die den Weg vom urbanen in den landschaftlichen Raum spürbar werden lässt.

Besonders künstlerisch überhöht wurde ein Wehr. Es ist als technologisches Schlüsselelement der Wasserbewirtschaftung in Form einer mit Cortenstahl verblendeten Stahlbetonkonstruktion betont und hebt sich durch seine horizontale Bänderung von der alten Fischhofbrücke ab.

Die neu ausgebildete Stadtkante westlich der Teichanlage erhält als Uferpark eine hochwertige Gestaltung. Private Hausgärten, die an den öffentlichen Park angrenzen, werden durch Hecken und Gehölzgruppen gefasst. Den Mittelpunkt dieser Stadtgärten bildet eine großzügige Park-Lounge, von der sich wiederum der Blick auf den Fischhof und die historische Steinbrücke öffnet. Entlang des Ufers dienen Steinstelen aus Theumarer Fruchtschiefer als außergewöhnliche Sitzgelegenheiten. Staudenbänder in warmen Farbtönen prägen die Bepflanzung der Stadtgärten sowie des gesamten stadtnahen Uferbereichs.

because this new bridge opens up views over the city and the landscape, in a circuit.

The landscape architects underscore their grand urban gesture of a new connection between the old town and the Fischhof Island by using a series of materials that illustrate the path from the urban area into the landscape area.

The weir was particularly artistically distinguished. It is emphasised because it is a technological key element of the water management system: a reinforced concrete construction lined with Corten steel. It stands out from the old Fischhof Bridge due to its horizontal banding.

The newly formed city periphery to the west of the pond area is given a high-quality design as a waterside park. The gardens of private houses bordering the public park are bounded by hedges and groups of trees. The focal point of these city gardens is formed by a spacious park lounge, from which a view opens up

Stadt berührt Park
City meets Park

Senkgarten
Sunken Garden

OBSTERNTE AUF DER FISCHHOFINSEL

Mittelpunkt des Fischhofparks ist das ehemalige Kloster Am Fischhof auf der Fischhofinsel aus dem 13. Jahrhundert. Das barocke Gebäude entstand um 1680 und wurde seitdem nur geringfügig verändert. Der Fischhof beherbergt heute das Amtsgericht Tirschenreuth.

Die ehemalige Klosterwiese wird von Wildblumen geschmückt und ist mit zahlreichen Obstbäumen bestanden. Die Besucher können hier Birnen, Äpfel oder Pflaumen pflücken, denn es geht in einem Park immer auch darum, den Nutzen der Natur in der Stadt zu vermitteln.

Ein beeindruckender Blick auf die Stadtsilhouette Tirschenreuths bietet sich vom Senkgarten aus. Dieser zwischen Teich und Fischhof gelegene Ort wird betont, indem die Landschaftsarchitekten die Platzmitte um einen halben Meter absenkten. Der Grundriss des mit Gräsern und Stauden bepflanzten Senkgartens verweist auf die ehemalige Gestaltung der Klostergärten. Eingefasst ist der Senkgarten mit dunkel-anthrazitfarbenen Platten aus Fürstensteiner Granit aus dem Bayerischen Wald. Die Verwendung von Baumaterialien aus der Region ist ein Prinzip von geskes.hack Landschaftsarchitekten.

Als grünes Pendant steht der Senkgarten dem steinernen Platz am See gegenüber und betont die städtebauliche Verbindung von der Altstadt zur Fischhofinsel.

ENTLANG DES UFERWEGS

Bei der Gestaltung des Fischhofparks hat der Schutz der Natur eine wichtige Bedeutung. Daher wurden Bereiche des neuen Stadtparks sehr zurückhaltend gestaltet. Ein Uferweg führt um den Teich und macht die oberpfälzische Kulturlandschaft zum Schaustück. So greift ein Storchenlehrpfad als Teil des Uferwegs den Artenreichtum dieser Landschaft auf. Ein Pavillon ist in der Schilfzone platziert und ragt über die Wasserfläche des Teiches hinaus. Von der Aussichtsplattform auf dem Dach öffnet sich dem Besucher der Blick in die Landschaft.

Dieser Pavillon ist eines von vier Bauwerken, die zugleich eine Reminiszenz an die alten Fischkästen sind als auch Landschaftsfenster, die einen Ausblick in den neu interpretierten Landschaftspark bieten. Die Pavillons helfen, die historischen Landschaftselemente zu „lesen".

Entlang des Uferwegs reihen sich weitere Zeugnisse der Tirschenreuther Kulturlandschaft wie der Mühlbach, der den ehemaligen Verlauf des Stadtteichs nachzeichnet. Entlang dieses Baches sind noch einige der typischen

to Fischhof and the historic stone bridge. Along the shores, stone stelae made of Theumar coloured slate serve as an exceptional seating area. Strips of shrubs in warm colour tones characterise the plants of the city gardens, as well as the entire shore area near the city.

FRUIT HARVEST ON FISCHHOF ISLAND

The focus of Fischhof Park is the former monastery Am Fischhof on Fischhof Island, dating back to the thirteenth century. This Baroque building was erected around 1680 and has only been slightly altered since then. Today, Fischhof accommodates the District Court of Tirschenreuth.

The former monastery meadow is adorned with wild flowers and has numerous fruit trees. Visitors can pick pears, apples or plums here. After all, a park is all about bringing the use of nature by people into the city.

An impressive view of the city skyline of Tirschenreuth is provided from the sunken garden. The area located between the pond and the Fischhof is emphasised by the landscape architects lowering the centre of this zone by half a metre. The layout of this sunken garden planted with grasses and shrubs references the former design of the monastery gardens. The sunken garden is framed with dark anthracite-coloured slabs of Fürstenstein granite from the Bavarian Forest. The use of building materials from the region is a point of principle for geskes.hack Landscape Architects.

The sunken garden stands opposite the stone Place at the Sea, providing a green counterpoint. It also emphasises the urban connection between the old town and Fischhof Island.

ALONG THE SHORE PATH

When designing Fischhof Park, the conservation of nature played an important part. The areas of the new city park were therefore designed in a very understated way. A shore path leads around the pond, showcasing the Upper Palatinate cultural landscape. In this respect, an educational stork trail, part of the shore path, reveals the wealth of species in this landscape. A pavilion is positioned in the reed zone, projecting out over the water surface of the pond. From the

Ehemalige Fischhofinsel

Former Isle of Fischhof

Platz am See
Place at the Lake

Sitzstufen am Seeufer
Stepped Seating at the Shore

Neue Verbindung zum Museumsquartier

New Link to the Museum's Quarter

Fischkästen erhalten geblieben, die von der traditionellen Fischereiwirtschaft der Region zeugen.

Nicht nur die Pavillons sind Anziehungspunkte im Seepark. geskes.hack schufen weitere Attraktionen wie zum Beispiel den Themenspielplatz „Fischers Fritz". Hier übertragen die Landschaftsarchitekten Bildmotive der Fischereiwirtschaft auf Spielangebote. Die Holzspielgeräte der als Wasserspielplatz konzipierten Landschaft sind künstlerisch gestaltete Unikate. Sie wurden eigens für diesen besonderen Ort entwickelt. So laden zum Beispiel eine bekletterbare Reuse sowie verschiedene Spielfische, teils als Wasserspeier konzipiert, zum Entdecken und Ausprobieren ein. Ein großer Königskarpfen bestimmt die Szenerie.

Und noch ein weiterer Spielbereich entstand im Zuge der Gartenschau: der Spielplatz „Fish'n Fun". Diese Anlage ist auf Ansprüche von Skatern und BMX-Fahrern zugeschnitten. Um diesen gerecht zu werden, suchten die Landschaftsarchitekten das Gespräch mit jungen Leuten aus Tirschenreuth und Umgebung, die ihre Erfahrungen und Ideen einbringen konnten.

Die Kombination der authentischen und historischen Landschaftselemente mit den zurückhaltend zeitgenössischen Architekturen der Pavillons macht den besonderen Reiz des Fischhofparks aus. geskes.hack Landschaftsarchitekten vermitteln mit wenigen, aber eindeutigen Zeichen zwischen der Stadtgeschichte und dem heutigen Landschaftsraum.

observation platform on the roof, the visitor has a view out over the landscape.
This pavilion is one of four structures that simultaneously offer a reminiscence of the old fish boxes and landscape windows that offer a view of the newly interpreted landscape park. The pavilions help to "read" the historical landscape elements.

Along the shore path, other testimonies to the Tirschenreuth cultural landscape can be found. These include the Mühlbach, which replicates the former course of the city pond. Along this stream, some typical fish boxes survive to bear witness to the region's traditional fishing economy.

The pavilions are not the only centres of attraction in the Lake Park. geskes.hack created other attractions such as, for example, the theme playground "Fisher's Fritz". Here, the landscape architects transfer picture motifs from the fishing industry to play facilities. Designed as a water playground, the pieces of wooden play equipment are artistically designed unique items. They were especially developed for this special place. In this respect, a weir that can be climbed up is inviting to discover and try out, as are the various toy fishes, partly designed as water spouts. A large king carp determines the scenery.

Another play area was created in the course of the garden show: the playground "Fish' n Fun". This complex is tailored to the demands of skaters and BMX riders. In order to do justice to them, the landscape architects held conversations with young people from Tirschenreuth and surrounding areas, who were able to contribute their experience and ideas.

The special attraction of Fischhof Park is due to the combination of authentic and historical landscape elements with the understated contemporary architecture of the pavilion. geskes.hack Landscape Architects convey few but clear signs between the city history and today's landscape.

Aussichtspavillon
Look-out Pavilion

Fischkästen als
Aussichtspavillons

Fish Boxes as
Look-out Pavilions

Holzsteg an der Storchenwiese

Wooden Bridge at Storchenwiese

Themenspielplatz
Fischers Fritz

Theme Playground
Fisher's Fritz

Spielreuse
Play Fish Trap

SEEPARK ZÜLPICH

Römische Badekultur
Roman Bathing Culture

Der Seepark Zülpich ist heute die Attraktion zwischen Rhein und Eifel, einer an natürlichen Seen armen Landschaft. Anlässlich der Landesgartenschau 2014 wurde Zülpich in Anlehnung an ihre Geschichte als „Stadt der Badekultur" entwickelt.
Als ein Markenzeichen verbinden geskes.hack Landschaftsarchitekten die Entwicklung attraktiver Freizeitanlagen mit dem Aufdecken vergangener Schichten. Diesen Schichten nähern sich die Landschaftsarchitekten gestalterisch durch besondere bauliche Elemente – und indem sie die städtebaulichen Zusammenhänge betonen.

Located between the Rhine and the Eifel in a landscape with few natural lakes, Zülpich Lake Park is the area's attraction today. On the occasion of the State Garden Show 2014, Zülpich was turned into a "City of Bathing Culture" based on its history.
In a trademark style, geskes.hack Landscape Architects combined the development of attractive leisure facilities by revealing layers of the past. The landscape architects approached these layers creatively through special structural elements – and by emphasising the urban contexts.

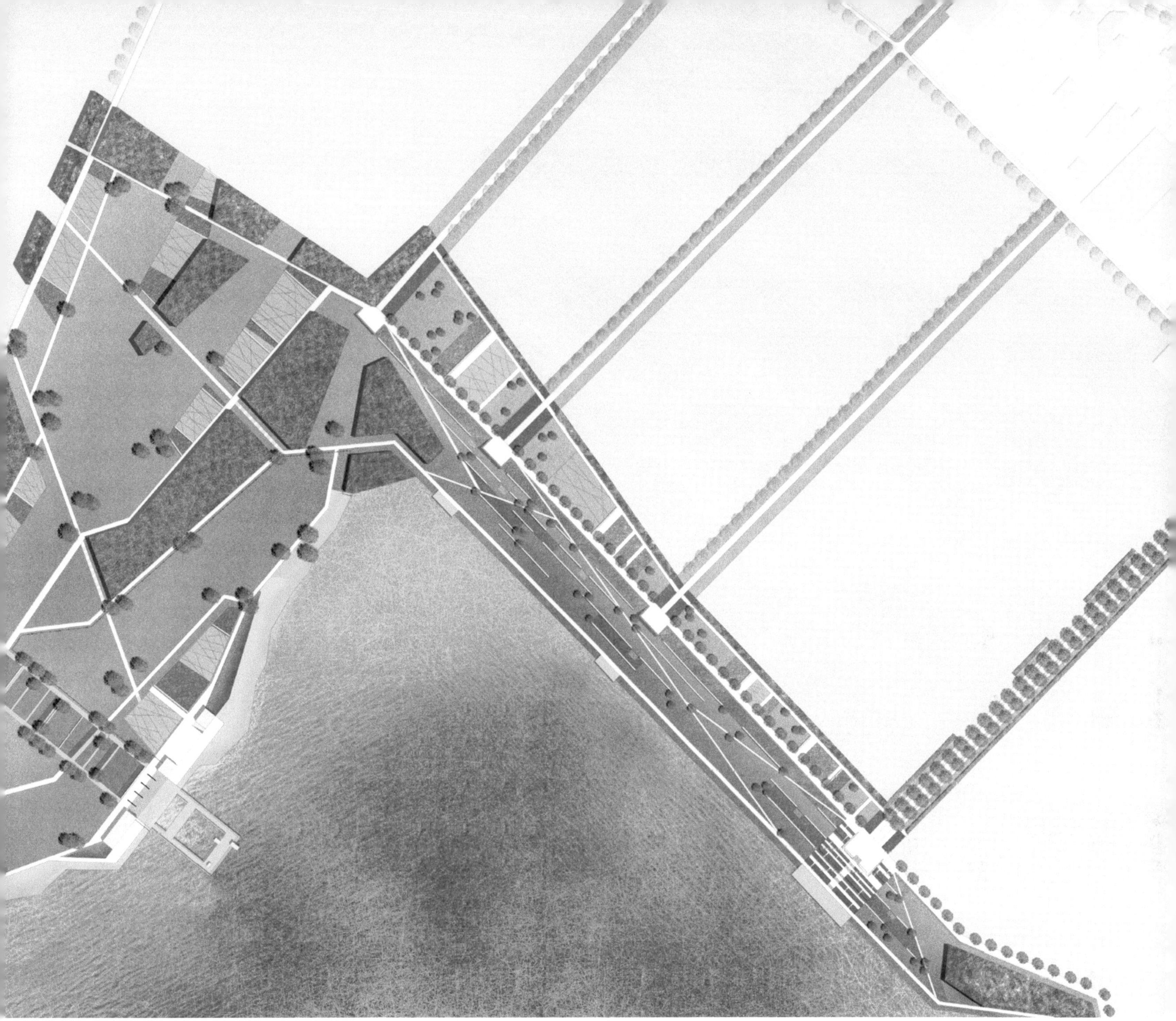

Landesgartenschau Zülpich 2014
Seepark Zülpich

Leistungszeitraum: 2011–2014
Leistungsphasen: 1–8
Fläche: 19 Hektar

Zülpich State Garden Show 2014
Lake Park Zülpich

Construction Period: 2011–2014
Construction Phases: 1–8
Area: 19 hectares

Blick vom Aussichtsbalkon an der Römerbastion

View from the Observation Balcony at the Roman Bastion

Uferplatz

Waterfront

Terrassen am ehemaligen Tagebau

Terraces at former Opencast Mine

GEOSTRATEGIE BERGBAU-FOLGELANDSCHAFT

Dass es in Zülpich gleich die römische Antike war, die freigelegt werden und als Inspiration für eine neue Landschaft dienen konnte, erwies sich gestalterisch und technisch als besondere Herausforderung.

Die Gründung Zülpichs geht auf die Römer zurück. Die Stadt am Kreuzungspunkt mehrerer römischer Handelswege war vor fast 2000 Jahren das größte Bad nördlich der Alpen. Natürlich ist das historische römische Bad, heute Herzstück eines einzigartigen Museums der Badekultur, nicht mit einer Wellness-Anlage heutigen Zuschnitts zu vergleichen. Römische Badekultur war Teil der Alltagskultur in allen Bevölkerungsschichten, das Baderitual war im gesamten Römischen Reich standardisiert.

Zülpich hat neben der römischen und mittelalterlichen auch eine jüngere Geschichte, und das ist eine typische Geschichte des 20. Jahrhunderts. Die Stadt liegt im Bereich des niederrheinischen Braunkohlenbeckens. Daher wurde am Rande der Stadt ab 1953 in zwei Tagebauen Braunkohle abgebaut. In diesen zwar technisch modernen, aber relativ kleinen Gruben erwies sich der Braunkohleabbau jedoch rasch als unwirtschaftlich, sodass er schon nach 15 Jahren wieder eingestellt wurde.

Der heutige See entstand im Rahmen der Rekultivierung des Bergbaugeländes. Vom vorgelagerten Aussichtspunkt , der einer Römerbastion nachempfunden ist, fällt der Blick auf den neuen Strandpark mit dem markanten Promenadendeck, das einer Badekultur des 21. Jahrhunderts Raum gibt. Der Zülpicher See ist nicht einfach nur eine Badestelle. Auf einer weit in den See hinausreichenden Plattform wird das Baden vielmehr inszeniert. Baden ist heute Sport, Erholung und immer auch ein Stück Selbstdarstellung. Die urbane Bühne auf dem See unterstreicht dies und knüpft an die ebenso traditionsreiche wie aktuelle Badeästhetik der Seebrücken, Badeschiffe und Strandpromenaden an.

Mit solchen neuen, auch großmaßstäblichen Aufgaben der Landschaftstransformation verbinden sich immer weitergehende Anforderungen an die Landschaftsarchitektur. Neben der Anlage repräsentativer öffentlicher Räume und funktionaler Freiräume für Sport, Spiel und Erholung sowie der Landes- und Stadtverschönerung durch Gärten und Parks bestimmen zunehmend regionalwirtschaftliche Interessen die Erwartungen an die Landschaftsarchitekten.

Städte im Transformationsprozess wie Zülpich suchen ihre Chance in neuartigen Industrie- und Bergbaufolgelandschaften. Die sogenannten „weichen Standortfaktoren"

GEOSTRATEGY FOR A POST-MINING LANDSCAPE

The fact that it was Roman antiquity that was exposed most immediately to serve as an inspiration for a new landscape in Zülpich proved to be a special creative and technical challenge.

The founding of Zülpich goes back to the Romans. This city at the intersection of several Roman trading routes was the largest spa to the north of the Alps almost 2000 years ago. Naturally the historical Roman baths, today the centrepiece of a unique museum of bathing culture, cannot be compared with a wellness complex design of today. Roman bathing culture was part of everyday culture for all social classes, and the bathing ritual was standardised throughout the entire Roman Empire.

As well as its Roman and medieval history, Zülpich also has a more recent history: a typical story from the twentieth century. The city is situated in the area of the lower Rhine brown coal basin. As a result, two open-cast mines have been worked on the periphery of the city from 1953. The mining of brown coal in these two technically modern but relatively small mines, however, quickly proved to be uneconomic. As a result, they ceased operations again after only 15 years.

Today's lake was developed in tandem with the recultivation of the mining site. From the upstream vantage point, which is modelled on a Roman bastion, one's eye is caught by the new beach park and its striking promenade deck, which provides space for a bathing culture of the twenty-first century. Zülpich Lake is not simply just a bathing place. Instead, bathing is presented on a platform stretching out far into the lake. Bathing is a sport today as well as a recreation, and always involves a touch of personal display. The urban stage on the lake underlines this and echoes the traditional bathing aesthetic as well as the current bathing aesthetic of the lake bridges, boats and beach promenades.

This type of new and large-scale landscape formation task imposes ever-increasing demands on landscape architecture. Besides the facilities for prestigious public space and functional free spaces for sport, play and relaxation and the need to create gardens and parks to beautify cities and administrative regions, regional economic interests are increasingly determining the expectations imposed on landscape architects.

Aussichtsbalkon an der Römerbastion

Observation Balcony at the Roman Bastion

Badesteg
Bathing Jetty

führen dazu, dass Städte und Regionen erheblichen Aufwand betreiben, um ihr Stadt- und Landschaftsbild zu pflegen und zu entwickeln. Dies zeigt sich auch in bautechnisch immer anspruchsvolleren Aufgaben.

Die Rekultivierung ehemaliger Bergbau- und Industrieregionen stellt ganz besondere Anforderungen. Aus Restlöchern werden Seenlandschaften, die von Landschaftsarchitekten nach ästhetischen Regeln gestaltet werden. Doch dazu müssen die Landschaftsarchitekten sich auch mit bodengeologischen Fragen, mit Setzungsfließen und mit Rütteldruckverdichtung befassen. Das ästhetische Wissen und das Wissen des Ingenieurs verbinden sich angesichts der Dimensionen neuer Landschaften auf eine neuartige Weise.

In Zülpich trafen drei Herausforderungen aufeinander: Angesichts der Dimension des Sees musste eine deutliche Geste die Stadt mit dem See verbinden. Zugleich galt es, die neue Stegkonstruktion auf dem See in einem Boden zu verankern, der durch Braunkohleflöze und Tonschichten gekennzeichnet ist. Entsprechend hoch waren die Anforderungen an die Gründungsstatik der neuen baulichen Elemente im Wasser. Nicht zuletzt war mit dem neuen Seepark ein großer Höhenunterschied zwischen Stadtgebiet und Seeufer zu überwinden.

BADEKULTUR

geskes.hack haben ihren Fachverstand als Landschaftsarchitekten verbunden mit dem Wissen von Wasserbauingenieuren und Geologen. Nur so konnte der Seepark Zülpich aus der Braunkohlelandschaft entstehen.

Um einen überzeugenden Bezug zwischen See und Stadt herzustellen und das Seeufer als städtischen Raum neu zu definieren, setzen die Landschaftsarchitekten auf starke Gesten: Die historisch nachgewiesene Achse einer alten Römerstraße, bepflanzt mit Säulenhainbuchen in Anlehnung an das mediterrane Vorbild von Zypressen, bindet als Allee die Innenstadt an den See an, wie eine Fuge in der neuen Landschaft. Sie mündet in die sogenannte Römerbastion, die Aussichtsplattform oberhalb des Sees, deren Stützmauern aus Naturstein bestehen. Eine Treppenanlage überwindet den Geländeunterschied der Uferböschung, flankiert von terrassierten Staudenbeeten. Eine terrassenförmige Holzplattform schließt die Achse auf dem Wasser ab.

Sichtachsen eröffnen den Blick auf die Weite des Sees, in die umgebenden Hügel der Eifel und auf das schräg gegenüberliegende Seebad, das eigentliche Highlight des Seeparks.

Seebühne
Lake Stage

Cities undergoing the transformation process, like Zülpich, are looking to innovative industrial and post-mine landscapes to generate opportunity. So-called "soft location factors" lead to cities and regions investing considerable amounts in order to maintain and develop their urban and rural landscapes. This is also demonstrated in ever more challenging technical tasks.

The recultivation of former mining and industrial regions poses very special challenges. They involve turning excavation holes into lake landscapes designed by landscape architects according to the rules of aesthetics. However, this also means that the landscape architects have to deal with questions of geopedology, with the sudden transition from a solid to a liquefied state, and with vibro-displacement. Aesthetic and engineering knowledge have to be innovatively combined to respond to the dimensions of new landscapes.

Zülpich offered three combined challenges: in terms of the dimension of the lake, a clear gesture was needed to connect the city with the lake. At the same time it was important to anchor the new bridge construction on the lake in a soil that is characterised by brown coal seams and clay layers. The static force demands on the foundations of the new water-based structural elements were correspondingly high. One significant aspect of this was the big height difference between the urban area and the lake that the new lake park had to overcome.

BATHING CULTURE

geskes.hack combined their technical know-how as landscape architects with the expertise of hydraulic engineers and geologists. Only in this way was Zülpich Lake Park able to emerge from the brown coal landscape.

In order to create a convincing link between lake and city and to newly define the lakeside as an urban space, the landscape architects deployed strong gestures: they used the known historical axis of an old Roman road, planting it with column hornbeams to echo the Mediterranean model of cypresses and creating an avenue connecting the inner city with the lake, like a transition into the new landscape. It flows into the Roman bastion, the observation platform above the lake, whose supporting walls comprise natural stone. A stairway flanked by terraced herbaceous borders

Barrierefreier Weg
zur Römerbastion

Barrier-free Path to
the Roman Bastion

81

KLEINE STADT MIT GROSSEM PARK

Insgesamt umfasst der neue Seepark Zülpich 20 Hektar. geskes.hack Landschaftsarchitekten konzentrierten sich angesichts der Aufgabe, einen großen Park für eine kleine Stadt zu schaffen, auf einige wesentliche, besonders starke Gesten, die den neuen Seepark identifizierbar machen. Zum einen ist dies die Fuge und Verbindung zwischen Stadt und See, die sich gestalterisch der Verknüpfung von Bäderkultur und Gartenkultur widmet. Zum anderen ist es die sinnfällige Erschließung des neuen Sees. Am Uferhang entstanden durch die Öffnung einer forstlichen Rekultivierungsfläche große Wald- und stimmungsvolle Gartenpakete, die sich zu einer neuen Landschaft fügen. Im Grunde handelt es sich bei dieser Parkanlage also um einen Landschaftspark, der die Geschichte des Ortes und das Freizeitbedürfnis im 21. Jahrhundert zu verbinden versteht.

overcomes the differences in terrain of the embankment. A terrace-shaped wooden platform concludes the axis on the water.

The visual axes open up a view over the expanse of the lake, into the surrounding hills of the Eifel and all the way to the lake resort diagonally opposite, the real highlight of the lake park.

SMALL CITY WITH A BIG PARK

In total, the new lake park at Zülpich comprises 20 hectares. To create a big park for a small city, geskes.hack Landscape Architects concentrated on some essential, particularly strong gestures that give the new lake park an identity. On the one hand, this is the transition and connection between city and lake, with a design dedicated to linking bathing culture and garden culture. On the other, it is the obvious way to develop the new lake. The opening of a forest recultivation area creates large parcels of forest and atmospheric garden on the river bank that turn into a new landscape. Basically, this park complex is a landscape park that understands how to combine the history of the location with the leisure needs of the twenty-first century.

Strandspielplatz
Beach Playground

Seepromenade

Lake Promenade

MARIENBERG / BRANDENBURG AN DER HAVEL

Kulturpark und Bürgerpark

Cultural Park and Citizens' Park

Durch die sensible Interpretation der Geschichte von Orten schaffen Landschaftsarchitekten *neue* Räume und Raumwahrnehmungen. Dass dabei manche alten Lage- und Funktionsbeziehungen wiederentdeckt und in zeitgenössischer Gestaltsprache neu interpretiert werden, dass Städte sich mittels dieser Landschaftsarchitektur ihrer Identität versichern, ist ein Kennzeichen der Arbeiten von geskes.hack Landschaftsarchitekten.

Thanks to their sensitive interpretation of this history of place, the landscape architects create *new* spaces and spatial perceptions. The fact that some old location-related and functional relationships are rediscovered and newly interpreted in contemporary design language, with the identities of the cities affirmed through the landscape architecture, is a hallmark of the work performed by geskes.hack Landscape Architects.

Bundesgartenschau Havelregion 2015
Sanierung des Gartendenkmals Marienberg in Brandenburg an der Havel

Leistungszeitraum: 2011–2015
Leistungsphasen: 1–8
Fläche: 12 Hektar

Federal Garden Show Havel Region 2015
Renovation of the Garden Monument Marienberg in Brandenburg an der Havel

Construction Period: 2011–2015
Construction Phases: 1–8
Area: 12 hectares

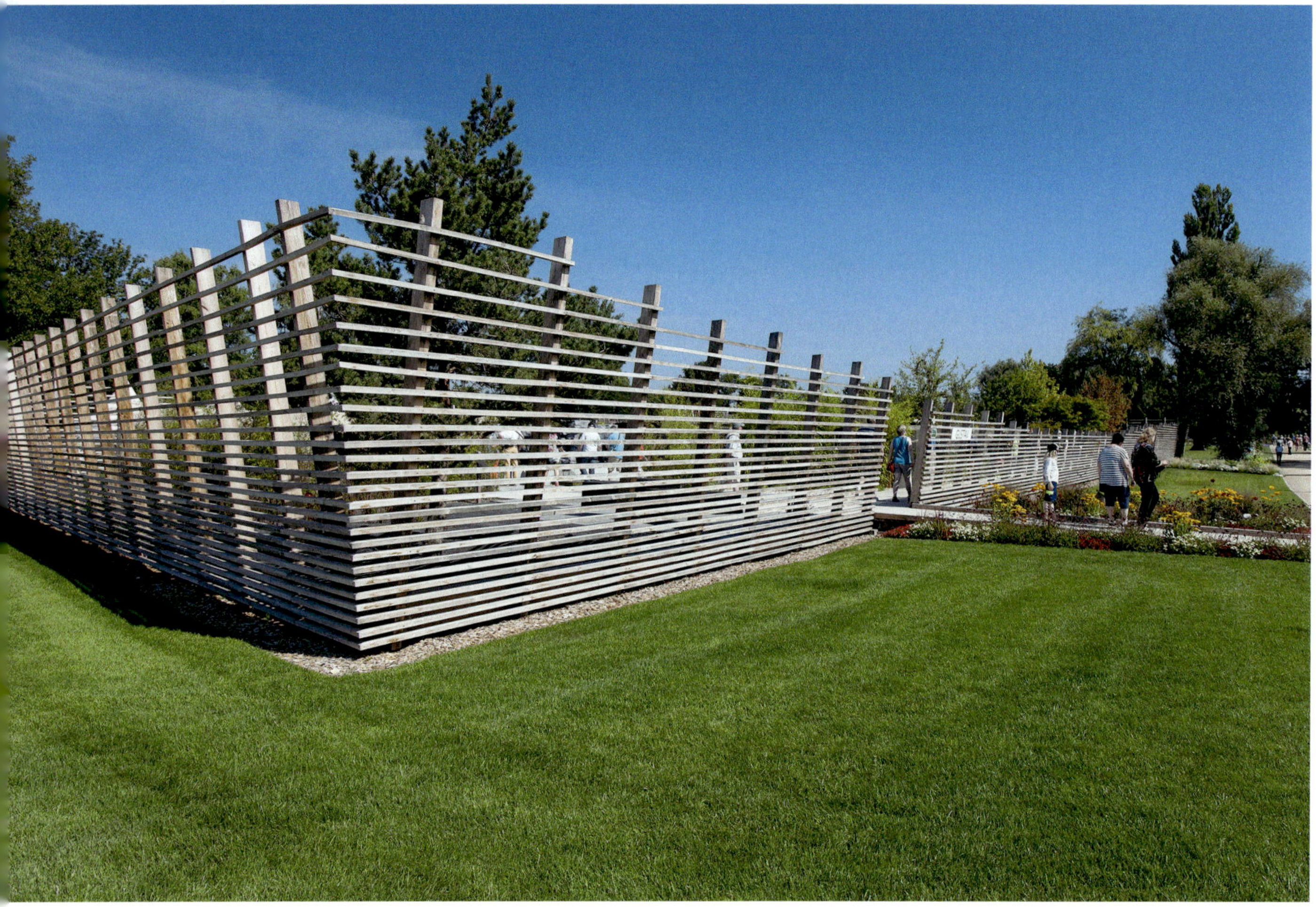

Packhofareal: temporäre Themengärten für die Gartenschau

Packhof Area: Temporary Theme Gardens for the Horticultural Show

STADT AM FLUSS

Die Bundesgartenschau 2015 empfing ihre Besucher in der Havelregion und vor allem in Brandenburg an der Havel, die sich zu diesem Anlass als „Stadt im Fluss" wiederentdeckte. Das am Ufer der Havel gelegene Packhofgelände bot als stadthistorisch wichtiger Ort einen geeigneten Platz für die Präsentation der gärtnerischen Ausstellungsinhalte der BUGA Havelregion. Die gestalterische Leitidee erinnerte an Schiffsrümpfe, die durch eine lichte Lattenstruktur nachgebildet wurden. Die Geschichte der Stadt Brandenburg ist eng mit dem Schiffsbau und den Transportwegen auf dem Wasser verknüpft. geskes.hack griffen diese Bezüge zur Schiffsbautradition auf und fanden neue, temporäre Bilder in Struktur, Mobiliar und Morphologie.

Der entscheidende Beitrag der Landschaftsarchitektur zur Zukunft der Stadt Brandenburg besteht jedoch in der „kritischen Rekonstruktion" des Marienberges, der als Park und Stadtberg die Havelstadt markiert.

TOWN ON THE RIVER

The Federal Horticultural Show 2015 welcomed its visitors to the Havel region and especially to Brandenburg an der Havel, which rediscovered itself on this occasion as a "Town on the river". As an important historical location, the packing yard located on the banks of the Havel offered an apt place to present the BUGA garden exhibition in the Havel region. The creative guiding principle brings to mind the hulls of ships, emulated through a clear lath structure. The history of the City of Brandenburg is closely linked with shipbuilding and transport routes on the water. geskes.hack picked up these references to the shipbuilding tradition and found new temporary images in the associated structure, furnishings, and morphology.

The decisive contribution of landscape architecture to the future of the City of Brandenburg, however, is found in the "critical reconstruction" of the

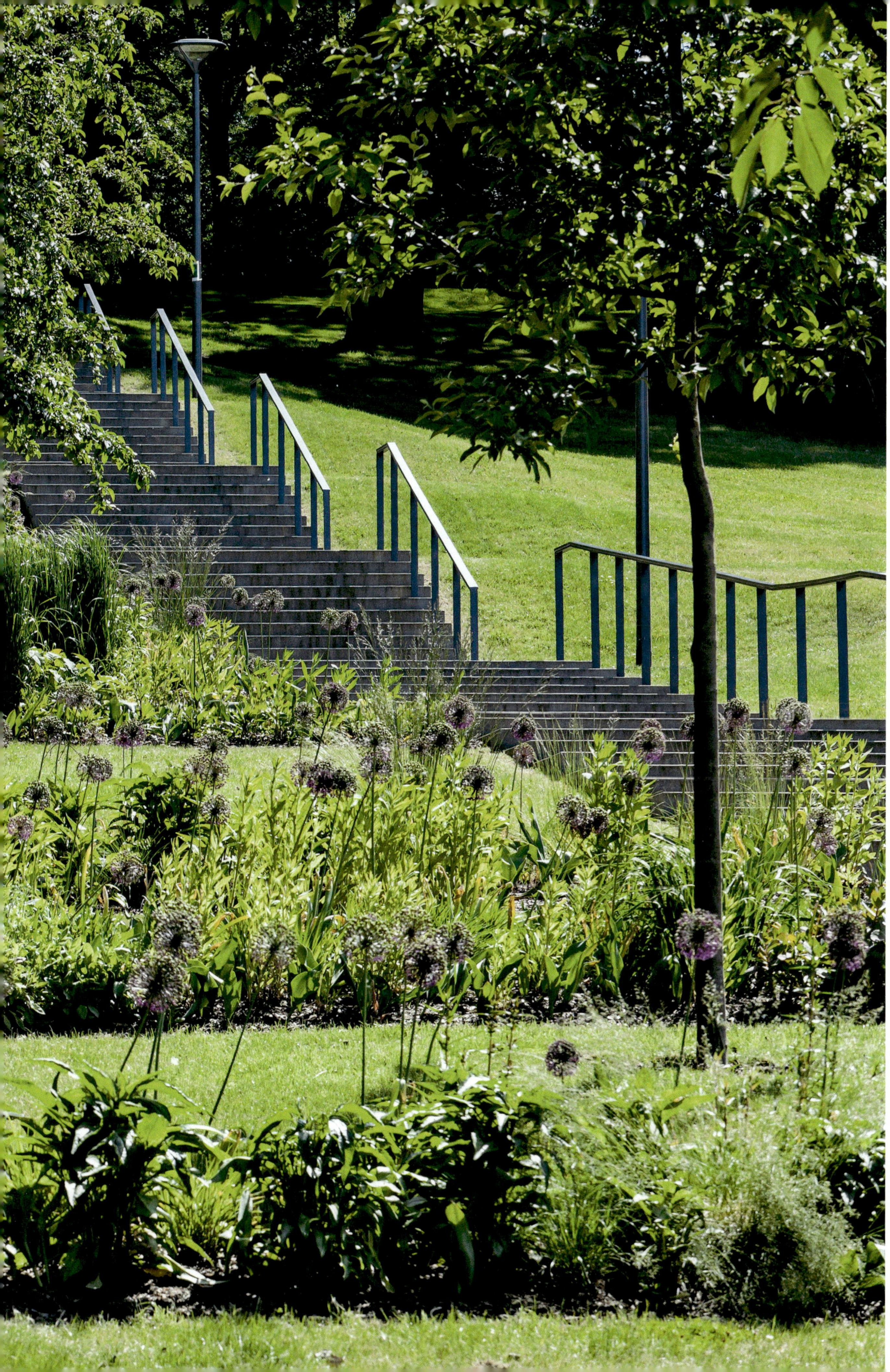

Hanggärten am Marienberg

Sloping Gardens at Marienberg

Dieser Hügel an der Havel, der sich nordwestlich der Altstadt Brandenburgs etwa 40 Meter über der Stadt erhebt, war schon zu Beginn des 20. Jahrhunderts als öffentliche Grünanlage konzipiert. Als Beispiel für einen Kulturpark aus DDR-Zeiten steht sie mit einer Gesamtfläche von rund 30 Hektar seit 1995 auf der Denkmalliste des Landes Brandenburg.

MARIENBERG-MYTHOS

Aufgrund seiner topografischen Exponiertheit war der Marienberg für die Brandenburger Bürger seit jeher ein besonderer, zeitweise sogar ein spiritueller Ort. Im Entwurf haben geskes.hack neben dieser Dimension auch die Besonderheiten eines Kulturparks erfasst, wie er für die DDR-Zeit typisch war.

Ein Panoramaweg entlang der oberen Hangkante verbindet heute die unterschiedlichen Architekturen auf dem Marienberg. Dazu bildeten geskes.hack Landschaftsarchitekten als starke Geste und Pendant zum historischen Südzugang Richtung Altstadt den neuen Nordzugang Richtung benachbarter Großsiedlung aus. Durch diesen und weitere barrierefrei gestaltete neue Zugänge hat der Park auch funktional gewonnen. geskes.hack haben den Park aus seinem Verhältnis zum Stadtraum heraus neu interpretiert und dabei zugleich Gartenpartien und das wichtige Parkplateau nach Maßgabe der Gartendenkmalpflege restauriert. Auf die Zeitschicht des Kulturparks wurde ebenso Rücksicht genommen wie auf die „Urplanung" des ehemaligen Leue-Parks. Bepflanzungen orientieren sich konsequent am historischen Vorbild. Nordhang, Aufgang Nord und der Panoramaweg als nun erstmals vollständiger Rundweg zeigen sich in Material und Dimension dagegen als Neugestaltungen.

Aufgrund dieser Überlagerung von Zeitschichten entsteht eine besondere Stimmung auf dem Marienberg, die die Kulturkolumnistin Ronja von Rönne zu der Überschrift „Ich war auf der Bundesgartenschau. Und es war schön" verleitete. Der Schlüssel zu diesem Erlebnis ist die Inszenierung der Ausblicke auf die Stadt entlang des Panoramaweges und seiner platzartigen Aufweitungen.

Die eigentliche planungsstrategische Leistung von geskes.hack Landschaftsarchitekten besteht aber nicht nur im Verweben von Kulturpark und Marienberg-Mythos, sondern auch in der Vernetzung mit der Stadt selbst. „Das strukturelle Problem des Marienbergs war seine räumliche Zurückgenommenheit gegenüber den angrenzenden Stadtquartieren aufgrund der trennenden Wirkung der am Rand angelagerten, privaten Nutzungen. Die konsequente

Marienberg, the city's hill and park that characterises the Havel town.

This hill on the Havel, which rises around 40 metres above the town to the northwest of the old town of Brandenburg, had already been designed as a public green area at the beginning of the twentieth century. As an example of a cultural park from GDR times, it has been on the monument register of the State of Brandenburg since 1995. It has a total area of around 30 hectares.

MARIENBERG MYTH

Due to its topographically exposed position, the Marienberg has always been a special and perhaps even spiritual place for the citizens of Brandenburg. Besides this dimension, in their design geskes.hack also captured the special features of a cultural park typical of the GDR period.

Today, a panoramic route along the upper edge links the different architectural features on the Marienberg. For this purpose, geskes.hack developed the new north entrance towards the neighbouring large estate as a strong feature and pendant to the historical south entrance towards the old town. Thanks to this entrance and other new accesses designed to be barrier-free, the park has also gained in functionality. geskes.hack have newly interpreted the park in view of its relationship to the urban area. This also involved restoring the garden areas and the important park plateau subject to historic garden regulations. The layers of the cultural park were taken into account and given equal status with the "original planning" of the former Leue Park. The planting is consistently oriented on the historical model. The north slope, the northern ascent and the panoramic route, however, have been turned into a complete circular route for the first time; their materials and dimensions make it clear that these are new creations.

The superimposition of layers of time creates a special mood on the Marienberg that inspired cultural columnist Ronja von Rönne to write the heading "I was at the Federal Horticultural Show. And it was great." The key to this experience is the staging of the views over the town along the panoramic route and its plaza-like expanses.

The real strategic planning achievement of geskes.hack Landscape Architects, however, is that

Rekonstruierte Blickachse vom Marienberg

Reconstructed Visual Axis from Marienberg

Pergolagarten auf dem Marienberg

Pergola Garden on Marienberg

Radweg auf den Marienberg

Cycle Track on the Marienberg

Öffnung des Marienbergs zur Stadt erfolgte durch die Anordnung neuer großzügiger Parkkorridore, die den Stadtpark barrierefrei bis an den Straßenring verlängern." Dort bilden kleine Stadtplätze neue Parkfoyers. Durch diese „Parkfinger" ist der Marienberg heute als Stadtpark mit der Stadt verzahnt.

Die Überlagerung aus neuem Parkentwurf, städtebaulicher Neubewertung, der Einbindung historischer Zitate wie dem Tanzplatz und der gartendenkmalgerechten Sanierung von Schlüsselbereichen des Kulturparks auf dem Marienberg zeigt, wie es geskes.hack Landschaftsarchitekten gelingt, durch sensible und sorgfältige Analyse das zu erschließen, was einen Park vor allem ausmacht: lebendige Vielfalt durch gestalterische Fantasie und viel Respekt vor Geschichte(n) und den Interessen der Gegenwart. Auf dem Marienberg wurde in Form des Panoramawegs eine neue stadträumliche Dramaturgie entwickelt und mit dem Respekt für die der Idee des Kulturparks sensibel zu einem neuen Bürgerpark verbunden.

they have not only interwoven the cultural park with the Marienberg myth, but have also interlinked it with the town itself. "The structural problem of the Marienberg was its spatial withdrawal from the bordering urban districts due to the separating effect of the private uses accumulated at the edge. The consistent opening up of the Marienberg to the town was done through the arrangement of new spacious park corridors that extend the city park, barrier-free, up to the city ring." There small town squares form new park foyers. Through these "park fingers", the Marienberg is today interlocked with the town as a city park.

The overlayering of the new park design, the urban revaluation, the integration of historical references like the dancing area, and the garden conservation restoration of key areas of the cultural park on the Marienberg shows geskes.hack Landscape Architects successfully developing the qualities that set a park apart through sensitive and careful analysis: lively diversity through creative fantasy and a great deal of respect for the history whilst serving the interests of the present. On the Marienberg, a new urban dramaturgy was generated by means of the panoramic route, sensitively combined with respect for the idea of the cultural park to create a new park for citizens.

„Parkfinger" führen in die Stadt

"Park Fingers" lead to the City

Gartendenkmalpflegerisch rekonstruierter Tanzplatz
Dance Floor reconstructed abiding by Garden Conservation Standards

Erlebnisspielplatz
Adventure Playground

STADTPARK WIESECKAUE / GIESSEN

Wissen im Park

Knowledge in the Park

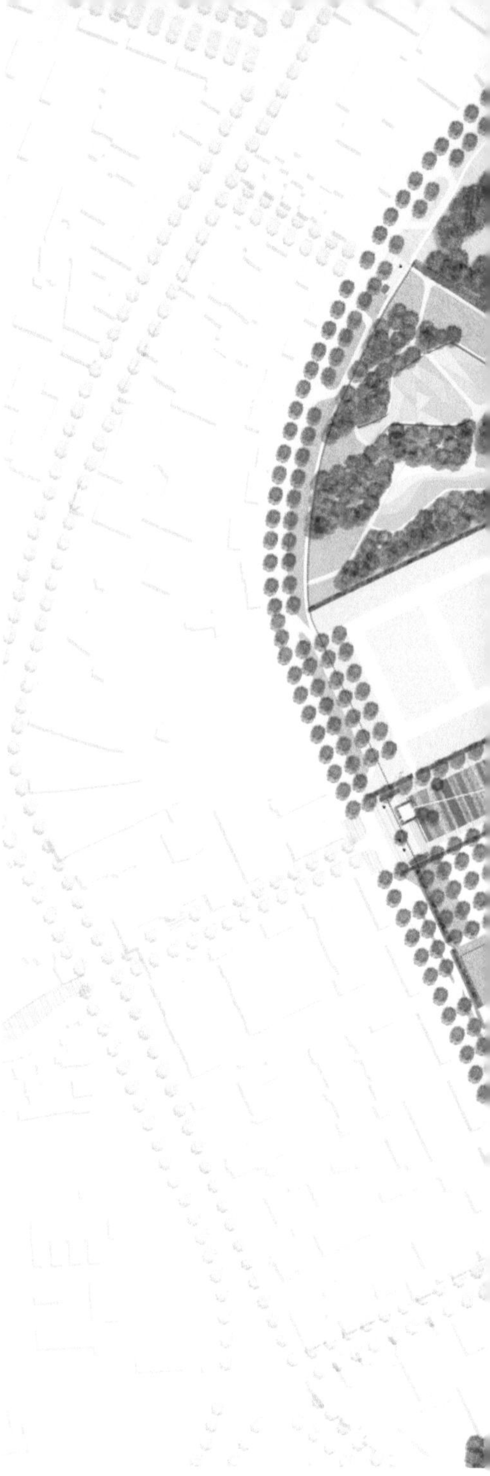

Die Beziehung von Gärten und Forschung ist das Merkmal des Stadtparks Wieseckaue in Gießen. Als Verbindung von Stadt und Landschaftsraum am Wasser entwickelten geskes.hack Landschaftsarchitekten die Wieseckaue, einen bestehenden Park im Nordosten der Stadt Gießen, weiter zum Wissenschaftsstadtpark. Dieses Parkerlebnis knüpft an die elementaren Stärken Gießens an. Zugleich erzählen die Landschaftsarchitekten die Geschichte der Wissenschaftsstadt Gießen auf neue Weise – als eine Geschichte im Park.

Wieseckaue city park in Giessen is characterised by the relationship between gardens and research. As a link between the city and the landscape zone close to the water, geskes.hack Landscape Architects turned the Wieseckaue, an existing park in the north east of the city of Giessen, into an urban science park. This park experience connects with the elementary strengths of Giessen. At the same time the landscape architects tell the story of the science city of Giessen in a new way – as a story in the park.

Landesgartenschau Gießen 2014
Stadtpark Wieseckaue

Leistungszeitraum: 2011–2014
Leistungsphasen: 1–8
Fläche: 23 Hektar

State Garden Show Gießen 2014
Wieseckaue City Park

Construction Period: 2011–2014
Construction Phases: 1–8
Area: 23 hectares

Platz am Neuen See
Space on New Lake

Steg am Neuen See
Bridge on New Lake

Neudefinition eines Gartendenkmals

New Definition of a Garden Monument

WISSENSCHAFTSPARK IN DER WISSENSCHAFTSSTADT

Gießen ist Bildungsstadt und Bildungsstätte. Die 1607 als Ludwigsuniversität gegründete, seit 1945 nach Justus Liebig benannte Universität sowie die Technische Hochschule Mittelhessen (THM) prägten und prägen die Stadt. Bei 76.000 Einwohnern beträgt die Zahl der Studierenden etwa 33.000 – mit 37 Prozent ergibt dies die höchste Studierendendichte in Deutschland – und jede Menge Parkbesucher. Wissenschaft wird in Gießen gemeinsam mit Kunst und Kultur als integrativer Motor für die Zukunft der Stadt begriffen.

Die Landschaftsarchitekten setzen auf die Bedeutung der Wissenschaft und finden zugleich ein beruhigendes Pendant in der Tradition der Gartenkunst in Gießen. Die Stadt galt im 19. Jahrhundert als „Gartenstadt" mit zahlreichen privaten, öffentlichen und universitären Gartenanlagen. 1609 entstand hier einer der ersten botanischen Gärten Deutschlands. Wo es anfangs um Sammeln und Systematisieren ging, entwickelte sich bald das Interesse am

A SCIENCE PARK IN THE SCIENCE CITY

Giessen is an educational city and an educational institution. Both the university (founded in 1607 as Ludwig's University and renamed in 1945 in honour of Justus Liebig) and the Technical University of Middle Hesse (THM) put their stamp on the city in the past as well as the present. With 76,000 residents, the number of students is around 33,000 – at 37 percent this means the city has the highest density of students in Germany. There are also plenty of visitors to the park. In Giessen, science joins with art and culture to provide an integrative engine for the future of the city.

The landscape architects based their design on the significance of science whilst at the same time finding a calming counterpoint in the tradition of garden art in Giessen. In the nineteenth century the city was considered to be a "garden city," with numerous private, public and university gardens. In 1609 one of

Optimieren. Die Naturwissenschaften wandelten sich vom reinen Sammeln hin zur Grundlagen- und dann zur angewandten Forschung. In Gießen tätige Forscher wie Liebig, Röntgen und die Gebrüder Humboldt beeinflussten, jeder auf seine Art, die Entwicklung der Welt.

geskes.hack haben sich in ihrem Entwurf zur Landesgartenschau 2014 dieser Geschichte gestellt. Und die Wissenschaft als Ideenwelt in einen Park der 1960er Jahre integriert. So kommt Gießen heute zu einem Stadtpark, der die Welt der Entdeckungen, die Welt der Pflanzen in der Kulisse der Wieseckaue spielerisch inszeniert. Über die Forscher verbindet die Landschaftsarchitektur das Abenteuer Wissenschaft mit dem Abenteuer der Expeditionen. Gemeinsame Triebkraft ist die Neugierde. geskes.hack knüpfen mit diesem Entwurf an eine 50 Jahre alte Gestaltung Günther Grzimeks an.

FORSCHUNG UND GARTENKUNST

Im Mittelpunkt steht heute nicht mehr, wie noch bei Grzimek, der Park als Freizeitraum für den Feierabend, sondern der Park als elementare Identität einer Stadt. Dabei betont die Landschaftsarchitektur Forschung und Wissenschaft nicht als nanomolekulare Reagenzglas-Anordnung aus Messreihen und elektronenmikroskopischen Wissensvermehrungsschritten, sondern als großes Abenteuer – eben das Abenteuer des Entdeckens im Park.

Die Wieseckaue als Park war in den späten 1920er Jahren von Heinrich Wiepking-Jürgensmann entworfen worden. Rund um den neu angelegten Schwanenteich, eine geometrisch geformte Regattastrecke, entstand ein Volkspark, der die Gedanken von Sport, Kraft und Volksgesundheit in sich trug. 1965 überarbeitete Prof. Günther Grzimek den Park, indem er Anforderungen der nach dem Wiederaufbau erneut stark wachsenden Stadt aufgriff und in eine neue Interpretation des Volksparks überführte. Ein Schlüsselwerk der 1960er Jahre und eine feinsinnige Parklandschaft, entspannt und erholsam. Wie in jener Zeit üblich wurden Freizeitfunktionen wie Schwimmbad und Sportplätze in den Stadtrandparks konzentriert – Abstandsgrün inklusive.

Mit ihrer Neudefinition knüpfen geskes.hack Landschaftsarchitekten respektvoll an die Planung von Grzimek an, definieren den Park in der Verknüpfung mit dem Thema Wissenschaft in seiner Bedeutung aber grundlegend neu. Aufbauend auf der starken räumlichen Grundstruktur wird der Park zu einer eigenständigen Aussage, zur Adresse in der Wissenschaftsstadt. Dafür überprüften die Landschaftsarchitekten im Detail jede einzelne Wegebreite, die

the first botanical gardens in Germany was built here. Initially, it was dedicated to collecting and systematising, but an interest in optimisation soon developed. The natural sciences changed from pure collecting to basic research and then to applied research. Researchers working in Giessen (such as Liebig, Röntgen, and the Humboldt brothers) influenced the development of the world, each in their own way.

geskes.hack engaged with this history in their design for the State Horticultural Show 2014. They also integrated the world of ideas offered by science into a 1960s' park. This is how Giessen turned into the city park of today playfully staging the world of discoveries and plants against the backdrop of the Wieseckaue. With the researchers as the key, the landscape architecture combines the adventure of science with the adventure of expeditions. The joint driving force is curiosity. This design by geskes.hack connects with a 50-year-old design by Günther Grzimek.

RESEARCH AND GARDEN ART

Grzimek's design focused on the park as an after-work leisure area; this is no longer the case today. Rather, the park is an essential part of the city's identity. The landscape architecture strategy doesn't emphasise research and science in the form of a nanomolecular test tube arrangement comprising measurement series and electro-microscopic knowledge enhancement steps. Instead, it emphasises science as a great adventure – quite simply, the adventure of discovery in the park.

Wieseckaue park was designed in the late 1920s by Heinrich Wiepking-Jürgensmann. Around the newly designed swan pond and geometrically shaped regatta course, a people's park was built, dedicated to the idea of sport, strength, and people's health. In 1965 Professor Günther Grzimek remodelled the park, responding to the greatly increased demands of the post-reconstruction city and transposing these into a new interpretation of the people's park. This is a key work of the 1960s: a subtle park landscape, relaxed and relaxing. As was typical at the time, leisure functions such as swimming pools and sports grounds were concentrated in city periphery parks – with greenery included for spacing.

In redefining this park, geskes.hack Landscape Architects connect with Grzimek's plans in a respectful

Parkfoyer: Campus am See
Park Foyer: Campus on the Lake

räumliche Wirkung aus Licht und Schatten entlang der Spazierwege, die Anordnung aller Gehölze und damit die Gesamtwirkung des beliebten Parks.

STRUKTUR UND STRATEGIE

Mit den Investitionen in den Park an der Wieseckaue wird eine nachhaltige Stadtentwicklung initiiert, die für einen erneuten Paradigmenwechsel steht: Die autogerechte Stadtstruktur der Nachkriegszeit wird zugunsten der Tradition einer neuen Gartenstadt revidiert. geskes.hack Landschaftsarchitekten öffnen daher die Stadt zum Park: Neu geschaffene Parkfoyers schaffen Blickbeziehungen zum Schwanenteich und öffnen den Hochschulcampus zum See.

Schließlich sind die städtischen Qualitäten im Exzellenzwettbewerb der internationalen Forschungs- und Wissenschaftsstandorte ausschlaggebend. Wie also bleibt eine Stadt für Wissenschaftsbürger attraktiv? Indem sich die Stadt mit dem Park verbindet und dieser spielerisch mit den Wissenschaften.

PARKFOYERS VERKNÜPFEN STADT UND PARK

Der 35 Hektar umfassende Stadtpark in der Wieseckaue wird mit den angrenzenden Stadtgebieten verzahnt. Dazu werden markante „Parkfoyers" intensiv gestaltet – darunter der neue Platz am See direkt gegenüber der Technischen Hochschule. Die Anlage dieser neuen Parkfoyers zur nachhaltigen Verbesserung der gesamtstädtischen Grünstruktur wurde durch die Verlagerung von Infrastrukturen möglich.

Die repräsentative „Wissenschaftsachse" bildet die Verbindung zur Innenstadt. Sieben dauerhaft angelegte Themengärten, die „Wissenschaftsgärten", überraschen mit der räumlich-gestalterischen Inszenierung wissenschaftsdidaktischer Ideen. Die Wissenschaftsachse ordnet den Stadtraum zwischen Messeareal und Freibad neu und gibt diesem Bereich ein neues ästhetisches Gewicht. Die Gärten entstanden in Zusammenarbeit mit den Hochschulfakultäten in einem studentischen Ideenwettbewerb, sie greifen das grundlegende Thema der Forschungen Justus von Liebigs auf: die „Leistungen" der Pflanzen und natürlichen Lebewesen für das System Erde. Eingefasst von hohen Hecken, gliedern die Gärten als grüne Separees die Wissenschaftsachse. Die Achse mündet am Neuen Teich in eine neu gebaute Brücke, die den Besucher in das Parkgelände hineinführt.

way, but they also fundamentally redefine the park by giving it a new meaning through the link to science. Building on the strong basic spatial structure, they make the park an independent statement, an address in the science city. For this purpose the landscape architects reviewed each individual path width in detail. They also reviewed the spatial effect of light and shade along the walking paths, the arrangement of all the trees, and the overall effect of this popular park.

STRUCTURE AND STRATEGY

Investment in the park on Wieseckaue has initiated a sustainable urban development that represents a renewed change of paradigm: the car-friendly urban structure of the post-war period has been revised in favour of the tradition of a new garden city. geskes.hack Landscape Architects therefore open the city to the park: newly created park foyers create views of the swan pond and open the university campus up to the lake.

Ultimately, it is urban qualities that are decisive in the competition of excellence between the international research and science locations. But how does a city remain attractive for citizens of the scientific world? The answer: by connecting the city to a park which connects in a playful way with science.

PARK FOYERS LINK CITY AND PARK

The city park in the Wieseckaue extends for 35 hectares and is linked to neighbouring urban districts by means of striking, intensively designed "park foyers" – including the new Platz am See (Place at the Lake) directly opposite the Technical University. The creation of these new park foyers, intended for the sustainable improvement of the overall urban green structure, was made possible through the relocation of infrastructures.

The prestigious "science axis" forms the link to the inner city. Seven permanent gardens, the "science gardens", present scientific doctrines in spatial, creative, and startling ways. The science axis reorders the urban space between the trade fair area and the open air swimming pool, giving this area a new aesthetic weight. The gardens were created in cooperation with the university faculties, with ideas developed through a student competition. They adopt the fundamental theme of Justus von Liebig's research work:

Am Neuen See
At the New Lake

Quellgarten
Spring Garden

Gräserpflanzung im Quellgarten

Planting Grasses in the Spring Garden

Aus dem nördlichen Stadtgebiet läuft der Quellgarten durch eine Kleingartenanlage bis in den Park hinein. Aufwendig gestaltet als in Cortenstahl gefasster Senkgarten mit Trittsteinen entlang eines kleinen Bachlaufes, gespeist aus einer natürlichen Quelle, besticht er atmosphärisch durch die besondere Pflanzenauswahl. Überkrönt von Silberweiden entstand ein naturnahes, dennoch gärtnerisches Feuchtbiotop. Die Topografie nutzend, öffnet der Quellgarten gleichzeitig den Blick auf die Hochschule über den Neuen Teich hinweg und fokussiert den Blick aus der Stadt in Richtung der Quelle.

ARTEFAKTE

Das Zentrum der Grzimek'schen Parkgestaltung ebenso wie des neuen Wieseckaue-Parks bildet der s-förmige, 6 Hektar große Neue Teich. Durch eine Halbinsel ist dieser kleinteilig in separate Bereiche mit wechselnden Uferszenerien untergliedert. Ein blühend gesäumter Rundweg entlang des Wassers, angelegt nach dem Prinzip des Beltwalks im englischen Landschaftsgarten, nimmt die organische Planung von Grzimek auf und bildet das neue Rückgrat des Parks. Diese Parkpromenade führt die Besucher durch abwechslungsreiche Landschaftsbilder, inszeniert durch neu geschaffene Blickbezüge quer über den See: Offene, sonnige Wiesen und Staudenpflanzungen wechseln mit dichten, schattigen Gehölzgruppen und schilfreichen Uferpartien. Der Rundweg erschließt – ebenfalls nach dem

the "contributions" of plants and natural organisms to the ecosystem. Framed by high hedges, the gardens divide the science axis as green screens. At the new pond, the axis extends over a newly built bridge that leads the visitor to the site of the park.

From the northern city district, the spring garden runs through the allotments right into the park. An elaborately designed sunken garden with stepping stones framed in Corten steel alongside a small watercourse fed from a natural spring is given a captivating atmosphere by the careful selection of plants. A natural yet horticultural wetland has been created, crowned with white willows. The spring garden makes use of the topography whilst opening up the view over the university beyond the new pond. It also focuses the view from the city in the direction of the spring.

ARTEFACTS

The s-shaped, 6-hectare new pond represents the centre of both Grzimek's park design and the new Wieseckaue park. A peninsula divides it into small separate areas with a variety of shore compositions. A flower-lined circular route along the water, created based on the principle of the belt walk in the English landscape garden, adopts Grzimek's organic planning and forms the new backbone of the park. This park promenade leads the visitors through varying

Gefasst in Cortenstahl –
im Quellgarten

Framed in Corten Steel –
in the Spring Garden

Skateanlage
Skate Park

Vorbild des englischen Landschaftsgartens – alle wesentlichen Attraktionen, wie das See-Café am besonnten Nordufer, intime Aufenthaltsplätze am Wasser, Spiellandschaften und Sportmöglichkeiten. Eingestreut in die weiten Wiesen liegen drei kraftvoll gestaltete Abenteuerspiel-Stationen, die als „Spielschollen" die Reisen Alexander von Humboldts zum Thema machen – sie heißen Orinoco, Chimborazo und Acapulco.

INTERAKTION

Mit farbenfrohen, zeltähnlichen Holzelementen und hölzernen Spielskulpturen wie einem Schiff, Schatztruhen oder einem riesigen Kletter-Ei vermitteln die Stationen des Spielplatzes „Humboldts Reise" den Spaß am Entdecken und Ausprobieren. Interaktion wird belohnt, aktive Besucher lösen Wirkung im Raum aus. So lassen sich Nebeldüsen durch Sportgeräte aktivieren.

Ein Teil der Wieseckaue ist als Natura-2000-Gebiet ausgewiesen. Der Schutz sensibler Uferbereiche auf dem

Humboldts Reisen: Spielscholle Orinoco
Humboldt's Journeys: Play Iceberg Orinoco

landscape pictures, enabled by newly created views across the lake: open, sunny meadows and perennial crops alternate with dense, shadowy groups of trees and shores rich in reeds. Also based on the English landscape garden model, the circular route accesses all the important attractions, like the Lake Café on the sunny northern shore, intimate places to linger by the waterside, play landscapes and sport opportunities. Scattered amid the wide meadows are three powerfully designed adventure stations. These are "play icebergs" with the journeys of Alexander von Humboldt as their theme – they are called Orinoco, Chimborazo, and Acapulco.

INTERACTION

With colourful, tent-like wooden elements and wooden play sculptures resembling a ship, treasure chests or a giant climbing egg, the stations of "Humboldt's journey" playground speak of the joy of discovery, of

Spielscholle Amazonas
Play Iceberg Amazonas

Kletter-Ei in den
Spielschollen Chimborazo

Climbing Egg in
Play Icebergs Chimborazo

SAUERLANDPARK HEMER

Konversion im Felsenmeer
Conversion in Felsenmeer

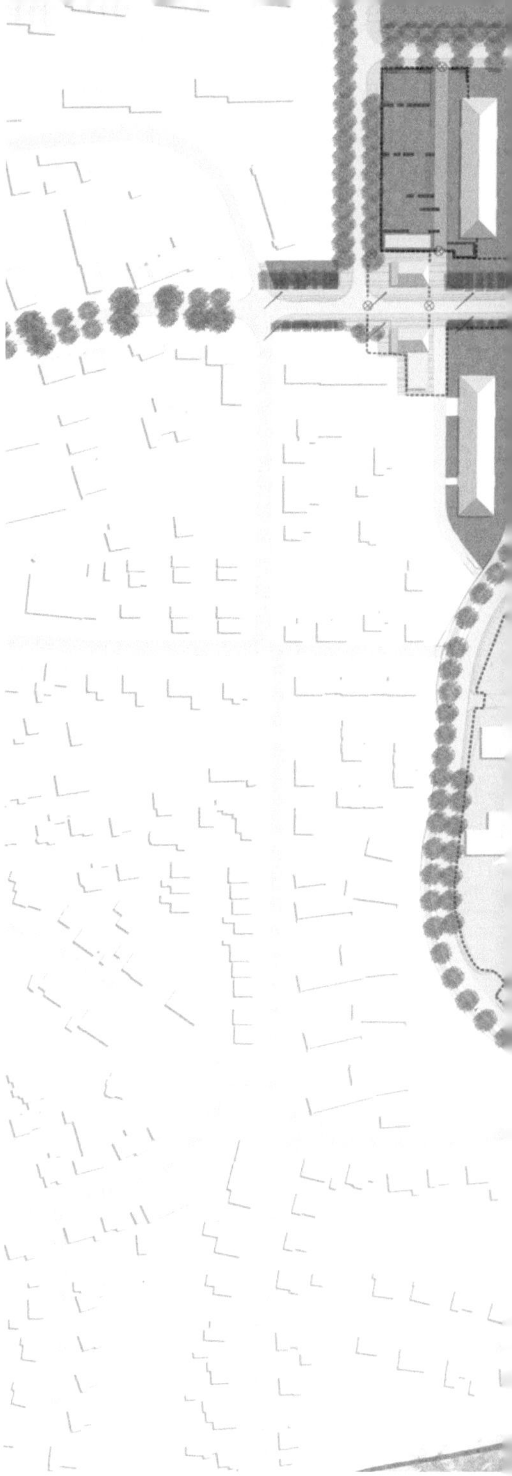

Ein Ort setzt der Landschaftsarchitektur die Bedingungen. Es gibt nicht zweimal denselben Ort, daher kann es auch keine Wiederholungen in der Landschaftsarchitektur geben. Hemer im nordwestlichen Sauerland setzt besondere Bedingungen. Hemer ist eine Stadt massiver Veränderungen. In der Heinrichshöhle kann man diesem Ort auf den Grund gehen.

The location sets the conditions for landscape architecture. No two locations are the same, therefore there can be no repeats in landscape architecture. Hemer in north-west Sauerland imposes certain special conditions. Hemer is a city of massive changes. The Heinrichshöhle (Heinrich's Cave) reveals to us the fundamental nature of this location.

Landesgartenschau Nordrhein-Westfalen 2010
Sauerlandpark Hemer

Leistungszeitraum: 2008–2010
Leistungsphasen: GP-Leistungen, 1–9
Fläche: 30 Hektar

State Garden Show North Rhine-Westphalia 2010
Sauerland Park Hemer

Construction Period: 2008–2010
Construction Phases: General Planning Services, 1–9
Area: 30 hectares

Zickzackweg zum Jüdbergturm
Zigzag Path Jüberg slope

Im Felsenmeer
In Felsenmeer

ORTE ENTWERFEN – GEOLOGIE UND TOPOGRAFIE

Wo wasserlösliches Kalkgestein im Laufe der Erdgeschichte ausgewaschen wurde, entstehen in sogenannten Karstgebieten unterirdische Flussläufe und Höhlensysteme. Die Heinrichshöhle ist eine dieser Höhlen in der weitgehend mit Wald- und Wiesenvegetation bedeckten Karstlandschaft des westlichen Sauerlandes. Im mit alten Buchen bestandenen Felsenmeer – eine wildromantische Landschaftsformation am Rande des Parks – findet diese Karstlandschaft ihren naturgeschichtlichen und landschaftsästhetischen Höhepunkt.

geskes.hack Landschaftsarchitekten waren gleich bei ihrem ersten Besuch vom Felsenmeer beeindruckt. Geologie und Topografie dieses Geotops bestimmen die Haltung der Gestalter zum Hemeraner Stadtpark, ebenso wie die stadtgeschichtlichen Bezüge im neuen Kulturforum die Gegenwart des Ortes als städtischer Schwerpunkt im Grünen bestimmen.

DESIGNING PLACES – GEOLOGY AND TOPOGRAPHY

Over the course of the Earth's history, water-soluble limestone has dissolved to form underground river courses and cave systems in so-called karst areas. Heinrich's Cave is one such cave in the karst landscape of western Sauerland, largely covered with forest and meadow vegetation. Adorned with old beech trees – a wild, romantic landscape formation at the edge of the park – Felsenmeer is the highlight of this karst landscape, both in natural history and aesthetic landscape terms.

On their very first visit to Hemer, geskes.hack Landscape Architects were impressed with Felsenmeer. The geology and topography of this geotope determine the approach of the designers in creating the Hemer city park, just as the civic history elements in the new cultural forum determine the presence of the place as an urban focal point in a green setting.

Skateanlage am Felsenmeer
Skate Park at Felsenmeer

So ist die aktuelle Konversion der Landschaft geprägt von den Eindrücken eines Landschaftsraumes, der mehrfach Umbrüche erlebt hat und dabei immer attraktiver wurde. Offene Inseln im Waldsaum, einst entstanden im Rahmen militärischer Übungen, wurden zum Erlebnisweg im neuen Park. Das Gesteinsbild des Felsenmeeres prägt die Gestaltung der Skateanlage. Und Orientierung im Raum bietet die Landschaft selbst, bieten starke Elemente wie der Jüberghang oder das Felsenmeer. Diese Orientierung im und am Raum wurde zum Motiv für die Wegeerschließung des gesamten Areals sowie für die Sinnesgärten und für den Heckenirrgarten.

Die Wege sind als Erlebnisfolgen inszeniert, wie beispielsweise der Zickzackweg den Jüberghang hinauf. Dabei ist es geskes.hack Landschaftsarchitekten gelungen, diese Wege sensibel in die geologischen und naturräumlichen Gegebenheiten einzupassen. Entstanden ist ein Waldsaum-Park als naturnahes Erlebnis.

Den Kontrast bildet die Himmelstreppe. Sie ist die bestimmende Geste des Parks. Eine starke Geste, die die Innenstadt über das neu entstandene Kulturforum mit dem Landschaftsraum des Sauerlandes verbindet

DER HIMMELSSPIEGEL

Hemer liegt inmitten der Mittelgebirgslandschaft des Sauerlandes, nur 30 Kilometer von Dortmund und dem Ruhrgebiet entfernt. Bergbau und Eisenverarbeitung hatten in Hemer ihre Hochzeit schon erreicht, bevor im Ruhrgebiet Schwerindustrie und Bergbau in großem Maßstab eine ganze Region neu definierten.

Daher suchte man in Hemer schon in den 1930er Jahren nach wirtschaftlichen Alternativen – und hoffte diese in der Entwicklung zum Militärstandort zu finden. Doch der 1936 begonnene Bau von Kasernen am Rande der Kleinstadt kam zunächst nicht zum Abschluss. Stattdessen wurden in Hemer Kriegsgefangene interniert. Das ehemalige Lager STALAG IV im Bereich des heutigen Parkgeländes ist ein für die Zeit des Nationalsozialismus und den Zweiten Weltkrieg wesentlicher Geschichts- und auch Gedenkort.

Ein schlichtes Metallkreuz inmitten des bewaldeten Jüberghangs erinnert seit 1947 an die Schicksale der Gefangenen. Vom neuen Jübergturm aus trifft der Blick unweigerlich auf dieses Kreuz. Und obwohl das Gedenken an das STALAG den neuen Park nicht prägt, besteht doch die Gelegenheit, sich in einer der ehemaligen Kasernen über die Geschichte des Lagers zu informieren. Das Kreuz im Wald und auch der Himmelsspiegel auf dem heutigen Kulturplatz,

In this respect, the current conversion of the landscape is characterised by the impressions of the landscape space, which has experienced several upheavals that have only served to make it more attractive. Open islands at the edge of the forest, created in connection with military exercises, became an adventure trail in the new park. Rock formations from Felsenmeer characterise the skate park. And the landscape itself offers orientation within the space, offering strong elements such as the Jüberg slope or Felsenmeer. This orientation within and in relation to space became the motif for the routes throughout the entire area as well as for the Garden of the Senses and for the hedge maze.

The routes, for instance the zigzag path up the Jüberg slope, are staged as experience sequences. geskes.hack Landscape Architects thereby succeeded in adapting these routes sensitively to suit the geological and natural conditions. What was produced is a forest edge park as a natural experience.

The contrast is formed by the Stairway to Heaven. It is the dominant gesture of the park: a strong gesture that links the city centre with the landscape of the Sauerland through the newly created culture forum.

THE SKY MIRROR

Hemer is located in the middle of the Sauerland low mountain landscape, only 30 kilometres away from Dortmund and the Ruhr area. Mining and iron processing were already present in Hemer before heavy industry and mining redefined a whole region on a large scale in the Ruhr area.

Thus, economic alternatives were already being looked for in the 1930s – and there was some hope of finding them by developing the location for the military. However, the building of barracks at the edge of the small city, started in 1936, was initially not completed. Instead, prisoners of war were detained in Hemer. The former STALAG IV camp in the environs of today's park site is a key historical memorial site for the era of National Socialism and the Second World War.

Since 1947, a plain metal cross in the middle of the forested Jüberg slope has called to mind the fate of the prisoners. Looking out from the new Jüberg tower, one's glance inevitably meets this cross. And although the commemoration of the STALAG does not

Himmelsspiegel
Sky Mirror

Blaue Stunde
am Himmelsspiegel

Blue Hour at
Sky Mirror

dem ehemaligen Exerzierplatz im Zentrum des Karrees der Kasernen, sind als Verweise auf diese Geschichte zu lesen.

Nach dem Zweiten Weltkrieg blieb Hemer bis zum Jahr 2007 Militärstandort. Heute ist diese Fläche Keimzelle für eine städtebauliche Arrondierung Hemers; der Park gibt hier Anregung und Rahmen: Anregung zur Ansiedlung attraktiver Wohngebiete am Hang und einen klaren Rahmen für diese Ergänzungsflächen durch den Park am Waldsaum.

geskes.hack Landschaftsarchitekten haben die Vergangenheit der Stadt Hemer in ihrer Arbeit wahrgenommen. So greift die Neugestaltung des Kulturforums, also des ehemaligen Exerzierplatzes inmitten der streng orthogonal angelegten Kasernen, die Tradition des Ortes auf. Das Forum, der neue kulturelle Mittelpunkt Hemers, bleibt in seinen Proportionen ein weitläufiger, streng gegliederter Platz, der die Geschichte des Ortes nicht verleugnet.

Einerseits ist ein Ort mit einem angenehmen Raummaßstab und einer urbanen Platzfassung entstanden, deren Gestaltung zum Ausruhen und Entspannen einlädt. Andererseits irritiert ein Wasserspiel, ein Wasserspiegel, der zeitweise ganz ohne Fontänen und Nebel einfach nur daliegt. Dieser Wasserspiegel – mit nur wenigen Zentimetern Überstauung ein wasserbautechnisches Kunstwerk – wird von den Landschaftsarchitekten als Himmelsspiegel bezeichnet. Von den Platzrändern und insbesondere vom Jübergturm aus erschließt sich diese Namensgebung. Tatsächlich wird

Himmelsspiegel auf dem Forumsplatz

Sky Mirror at Forum Square

characterise the new park, opportunities still exist to find out about the history of the camp in one of the former barracks. The cross in the forest is to be read as a references to this history, as is the sky mirror, the former parade ground in the centre of the barrack's square, today a cultural arena.

After the Second World War, Hemer remained a military location until 2007. Today, this area is a nucleus for an urban realignment of Hemer; the park offers stimulus and a framework: a stimulus for developing attractive residential areas on the slope and a clear framework for these additional areas in the form of the park at the edge of the forest.

In their work, geskes.hack Landscape Architects acknowledge the past of the city of Hemer. This is how the new design of the cultural forum (the former parade ground in the middle of the strictly orthogonally designed barracks) responds to the tradition of the location. In terms of proportion, the forum, the new cultural highlight of Hemer, remains a vast, strictly separate location that does not deny the history of the place.

On the one hand, a place with a pleasant spatial scale and an urban frame has been created, whose design invites one to slow down and relax. On the other, the water feature is provocative: a level expanse of water that in part simply lies there, completely without fountains. This water surface – a hydraulic engineering

jeweils für kurze Zeit der Himmel über Hemer in diesem Wasserspiegel sichtbar, bis wieder das Programm der Wasserspiele einsetzt oder ein vorwitziger Parkbesucher durch das Wasser zu gehen versucht.

Es ist konsequent, die Geschichte des Standortes in der Landschaftsarchitektur zu verankern, ohne sie zur Dominante zu erklären. Denn Hemer sucht mit dem im Zuge einer Landesgartenschau entstandenen Park ja gerade nach einem zivilgesellschaftlichen Anschluss an die militärische Tradition. Vielleicht wird manchem beim Blick vom Jübergturm auf den Himmelsspiegel die Doppelbödigkeit dieses Ortes deutlich, der heute so ungestört Freude erzeugen und ausstrahlen darf.

DIE HIMMELSTREPPE

Die Topografie als Leitmotiv des Entwurfs für die Himmelstreppe hat kunstgeschichtliche Bezüge, so in der Gartenkunst der Renaissance, und zugleich einen Bezug zur Geschichte des Standortes.

Die Geste der Treppe selbst ist streng. Zudem thematisieren die begleitenden Messmarken und die in Cortenstahl gefassten kleinen Balkone das Thema der Landvermessung und Landnahme. Der kontrastierende Zickzackweg, der diese Treppe immer wieder schneidet und letztlich auch zum Ziel führt, macht die Strenge der Treppe erst richtig deutlich. Denn dieser Weg ist ein dem Landschaftsraum angepasstes Bauwerk, während die Treppe den Landschaftsraum aufbricht. Durch die Geradlinigkeit der Treppe schufen die Landschaftsarchitekten eine Sichtachse zur Innenstadt.

DIE KANTE – STÄDTEBAU UND LANDSCHAFT

Bis heute ist die Metallverarbeitung, sind besonders Draht und Drahtprodukte, Messinghalbzeug, Badausstattungen und -armaturen ein wichtiger Industriezweig der Region. Doch beeinflusst die Metallindustrie das Landschaftsbild vor allem kleinteilig. Anders als im benachbarten Ruhrgebiet sind es die Landschaft, die umliegenden Höhenzüge, die die Hemer prägen, und nicht umgekehrt. Das Stadtbild ist das einer industrialisierten Kleinstadt, das Landschaftsbild jedoch entspricht dem einer Mittelgebirgslandschaft mit vielen naturräumlichen Reizen. Die Stadtkante, der Übergang aus der Stadt in die Landschaft, ist der besondere Reiz Hemers. Als Stadt am Hang vermittelt Hemer ein neues Bild von sich, eine neue Betonung ihrer Lage.

work of art flooded to a depth of just a few centimetres – is described by the landscape architects as a sky mirror – so named with reference to the plaza's periphery, and, in particular, the Jüberg tower. The sky above Hemer does in fact become visible in this expanse of water for a short time, until the water feature programme starts again or a cheeky park visitor attempts to walk through the water.

It is consistent to anchor the history of the place in landscape architecture without making it the dominant factor. After all, what Hemer is particularly looking for from the park created in the course of the state garden show is a civic connection to the military tradition. Maybe the ambiguity of this place will dawn on some people when looking down from the Jüberg tower to the sky mirror, which is allowed to generate and radiate joy today without interruption.

THE STAIRWAY TO HEAVEN

The topography-related leitmotif of the stairway to heaven design features art-historical references, such as the garden art of the Renaissance. At the same time, it references the history of the location.

The gesture of the stairway itself is severe. Additionally, it is accompanied by measuring marks and small balconies framed in Corten steel, which reference the issue of land surveying and land seizure. The contrasting zigzag route that keeps on cutting through this stairway and ultimately also leads to the destination makes the severity of the stairway very plain by contrast: this route is a structure adjusted to the landscape, whereas the stairway breaks up the landscape. With this linear stairway, the landscape architects have created a visual axis running straight to the town centre.

THE PERIPHERY – URBAN DEVELOPMENT AND LANDSCAPE

To date metal processing, in particular wire and wire products, brass semi-finished products, bathroom accessories and fixtures have been an important industrial sector for the region. Yet the metal industry influences the landscape image, particularly on a small scale. In contrast to the neighbouring Ruhr area it is the landscape, the surrounding range of hills that characterise Hemer and not the other way round. The

Himmelstreppe
Stairway to Heaven

Gärten an der Himmelstreppe
Gardens at the Stairway to Heaven

Stadtterrasse
City Terrace

Jede Stadt (ent)steht in Relation zu der Landschaft, die sie umgibt. Durch den Buchenwald im Bereich des Felsenmeers bietet die Hemeraner Landschaft einen schönen Bezug zu der mitteleuropäischen Naturlandschaft und somit eine Vielzahl an landschafts- und erdgeschichtlichen Bezügen. Für den neuen Park waren diese Bezüge Verpflichtung, mittels der Landschaftsgestaltung galt es, diese Bezüge durch eine Intensivierung der Sinneserlebnisse zu entdecken und zu stärken.

TRAINING DER SINNE

Der neue Park in Hemer lädt ein zur Auseinandersetzung mit der Natur, mit der Geologie, mit der Erdgeschichte sowie mit der Geschichte der Region und des Ortes. Die in den Park und das Kulturforum eingewobenen Erinnerungen und Überraschungen erschließen sich nicht immer auf den ersten Blick. Daher lädt der Park zu einem Training der Sinne ein, macht er die Orientierung im Raum ebenso zum Thema wie die Geschichte dieses Ortes.

geskes.hack Landschaftsarchitekten haben einen Höhepunkt dieses Sinnestrainings mit den Gärten der Sinne geschaffen, die quasi die Schleuse bilden hinein aus dem Waldhang in die ganz außergewöhnliche, schroffe und zugleich wildromantische Landschaft des Felsenmeers.

Um das Felsenmeer auf sich wirken lassen zu können, ist ein Parcours für das Sinnestraining eine gute Vorbereitung. Und da das Felsenmeer ein Stück Bergbaugeschichte und damit Wirtschaftsgeschichte der Region ist, wird dieses Thema in den Gärten der Sinne vorbereitet. Reminiszenzen an die Stadtgeschichte und die Wirtschaft stehen dabei im Mittelpunkt.

Metallverarbeitung als eine traditionsreiche Wirtschaft im Sauerland brachte die Drahtziehereien hervor, die typisch sind für die kleinen Städte der Region. Einer der Sinnesgärten stellt daher überdimensionale Drahtbürsten dar und verweist auf diese regionale Tradition.

Aus Metall sind auch die Zimbeln, die zu jedem Schlagzeug gehören. Zimbeln sind legendär in der Geschichte der klassischen wie der Popmusik. Daher wurde ihnen in Hemer ein Garten gewidmet. Der Wind streicht in diesem von Kornelkirschenhecken umgrenzten Garten durch die vielen Zimbeln, die auf unterschiedlich hohen Gestellen platziert sind. Ein ständiger Klangteppich umfängt die Besucher, die auch selbst in die Komposition des Windes eingreifen können. Ein meditativer Ort.

Orientierung sucht man auch im Streichholzgarten, in dem übermenschlich große Streichhölzer an einem Gestell

cityscape is that of an industrialised small town; the landscape, however, corresponds to that of a low mountain landscape with many natural attractions. The city edge, the transition from the city to the landscape, is a particular attraction of Hemer. As a city on a slope, Hemer conveys a new image of itself, a new emphasis on its location.

Each city emerges in relation to the landscape that surrounds it. Through the beech forest in the area of the sea of rocks, the Hemer landscape offers a beautiful reference to the central European natural landscape and with this a variety of landscape and geological references. These references were mandatory for the new park; through the landscape design it was possible to discover and strengthen these references through intensifying the sensory experiences.

TRAINING THE SENSES

The new park in Hemer invites visitors to become acquainted with nature and with geology; with the geological history and the history of the region and the place. The memories and surprises woven into the park and the cultural forum are not always apparent at first glance. Thus, the park invites visitors to train their senses, making orientation within space a part of its theme, along with the history of this location.

geskes.hack Landscape Architects have taken this training of the senses to a high level with the Garden of the Senses. It provides, as it were, an airlock between the forest slope and the extraordinary, craggy and at the same time wildly romantic landscape of Felsenmeer.

A route for training the senses is a good preparation for experiencing the full effect of Felsenmeer. And since Felsenmeer is also a piece of mining history and thus of the economic history of the region, this theme is also prepared for in the Gardens of the Senses. The focus is on recollections of the urban history and economy.

The longstanding Sauerland metal processing industry gave birth to the wire-drawing industries typical of the small towns in the region. One of the Gardens of the Senses is therefore an image of an oversized wire brush: a reference to this regional tradition.

Cymbals - part of every drum set - are also made of metal. Cymbals are legendary in the history of classical as well as pop music. This is why Hemer has

Streichholzspiel
im Park der Sinne

Match Game in
the Park of Senses

Klanggarten
Sound Garden

Im Hans-Prinzhorn-Irrgarten

In the Hans-Prinzhorn maze

Gärten der Bewegung

Gardens of Movement

hängen, quasi ein Streichholzbriefchen, durch das sich die Besucher langsam und unter ständiger Verschiebung der Verhältnisse, also der Streichhölzer, einen Weg zur Mitte und wieder hinaus zu bahnen versuchen.

DAS FELSENMEER

Eine Wunderwelt auf etwas mehr als einem Quadratkilometer – das Felsenmeer fasziniert Naturinteressierte, Geologieexperten und alle Besucher jeden Alters.

Der Blick in die prähistorischen Ursprünge menschlicher Besiedelung ist zugleich ein Blick in eine Sagen- und Märchenwelt. In dem von Farnen und Moosen bewachsenen Felsengeotop sind solche Fantasien naheliegend. Eine besondere Stimmung umfängt einen an diesem Ort, der selbst im Jahr der Gartenschau ein stiller Ort des Rückzugs blieb.

Doch was so aussieht wie ein Stück vormenschliche Wildnis, ist ein Produkt des vor- und frühindustriellen Bergbaus. Wo Erze abgebaut wurden, blieb ein Felsengewirr zurück, das heute wildromantisch wirkt. Bäume und Farne bilden ein schattenreiches Biotop mit vielen Vogelstimmen und Kleintieren.

Ein kleiner Rundgang durch das Felsenmeer und auch weiter zur Heinrichshöhle ist ein beruhigend wirkender Höhepunkt des Parkbesuchs. Das Naturschauspiel wirkt als größtmöglicher Kontrast zum neuen lebendigen Kulturzentrum am Stadtrand Hemers. Eine kleine Brücke über das Felsenmeer erlaubt ungewohnte Einblicke in eine Landschaftsminiatur, die für die Konversion und Neudefinition der Stadtrandlandschaft der sauerländischen Kleinstadt Hemer ein gestalterisches und atmosphärisches Vorbild ist. Gespeist wird dieser Wandel im Park der Gegenwart aus landschaftlichem Reichtum

a garden dedicated to them. The wind rustles through this garden surrounded by its hedges of cornelian cherry bushes, and blows through the many cymbals that are placed on frames of different heights. A constant soundscape surrounds the visitors, who can also intervene themselves in this composition played by the wind. This is a meditative place.

Visitors also look for orientation in the matchstick garden in which super-sized matches hang on a frame. This is a kind of little note made up of matchsticks, through which visitors try to find their way to the middle and out again, slowly and under constantly changing conditions.

FELSENMEER

A magic world within an area of just over a square kilometre, Felsenmeer fascinates those interested in nature, geology experts and visitors of all ages.

To look at the prehistoric origins of human settlement is also to look at a world of sagas and fairy tales. In the rock geotope covered in ferns and moss, these fantasies are obvious. A special atmosphere surrounds one in this place. Even in the year of the garden show, it remained a quiet place to retreat to.

However, what looks like a piece of pre-human wilderness is in fact a product of pre- and early industrial mining. The confusion of rocks that remains where ores were mined appears wild and romantic today. Trees and ferns form a shady biotope with many song birds and small animals.

A brief circuit through Felsenmeer, or a walk further towards Heinrich's Cave is both relaxing and a highlight of a visit to the park. The natural spectacle seems to be the greatest possible contrast to the new, lively cultural centre at the periphery of Hemer. A small bridge over Felsenmeer allows unusual insights into a landscape miniature that is a creative and atmospheric model for the conversion and redefinition of the landscapes on the outskirts of the small Sauerland city of Hemer. This transformation of the present day park springs from the wealth of the landscape.

Felsenmeer
Felsenmeer

Wasserspielplatz
Water Playground

BÜRO UND TEAM
PRACTICE AND TEAM

GESKES.HACK LANDSCHAFTSARCHITEKTEN

Eine besondere Genauigkeit des Sehens und Gestaltens von Räumen und Orten zeichnet die Landschaftsarchitektur aus dem Büro geskes.hack aus. Diese Genauigkeit ermöglicht einen bis ins Detail stimmigen Zusammenklang von Pflanzungen und Geländeformationen, von Infrastrukturen, Material, Mobiliar und Farbstimmungen. Selbstzweck sind diese Stimmungen der Landschaft nicht. geskes.hack Landschaftsarchitekten unterstützen mit ihrer Art, Landschaften zu gestalten, die Erzählungen von Geschichten, die sich aus dem Ort hervorbringen lassen. Dabei übernimmt das Spielen in den Arbeiten von geskes.hack Landschaftsarchitekten eine Schlüsselrolle, um Orte zu anziehenden Orten, zu Attraktionen zu entwickeln. Da dies in einer selbstverständlichen Buntheit der Landschaft passiert, schaffen geskes.hack alltagsschöne Stadt- und Landschaftsräume aus der jeweiligen Situation heraus. Das Können der Landschaftsarchitekten verbindet sich in bester Art und Weise mit den Talenten der jeweils zu betonenden Landschaft – ob im Karst des Sauerlandes, am Ufer des Schweriner Sees, an der zurückgewonnenen Aue des Raumbachtals im Vogtland, dem Trümmerberg im Osten Berlins oder am einstmals klösterlichen Fischteich in der Oberpfalz.

Ihr Talent, einen Raum exakt zu lesen und schöner denn je zu erzählen, haben geskes.hack Landschaftsarchitekten in vielen erfolgreichen Wettbewerbsbeiträgen und stimmigen baulichen Umsetzungen vom Main bis zur Spree vielfach bewiesen. Dabei gelingt es ihnen immer wieder, nicht nur räumliche, sondern auch zeitliche Entwicklungen der Städte und Regionen ins Bild zu rücken. Es entstehen Parks der Gegenwart. Gegenwärtige Landschaften.

GESKES.HACK LANDSCAPE ARCHITECTS

The landscape architecture produced by geskes.hack Landscape Architects is distinguished by a particular accuracy in seeing and designing spaces and locations. This accuracy enables a harmony of planting and landscape formations with elements of infrastructure, materials, furnishings, and colour schemes down to the finest detail. Nor are these landscape moods an end in themselves. The geskes.hack Landscape Architects' style of designing landscapes enables the relating of the tales that can be created from a place. As a part of this, play has a key role in geskes.hack Landscape Architects' work of turning locations into attractive places, into attractions. This is done by connecting with the natural colourfulness of the landscape; thus, geskes.hack create everyday beautiful urban and landscape spaces from the specific situation. This involves optimally combining the skills of the landscape architects with the talents of the specific landscape that is being emphasised – the karst landscape of the Sauerland, the banks of Lake Schwerin, the recovered floodplains of the Raumbach valley in Vogtland, the Trümmerberg (rubble mound) in the east part of Berlin, or the former monastic fish pond in Upper Palatinate.

On numerous occasions and in many successful competition entries and harmonious structural implementations of locations everywhere from the River Main to the Spree, geskes.hack Landscape Architects have proven their talent for accurately reading a space and conveying its story more beautifully than ever before. In doing so, they have been successful time and again in presenting not only the spatial but also the temporal developments of cities and regions. Thus, they create parks for the present day. These are present landscapes.

Kristina Hack und Christof Geskes

MITARBEITER
EMPLOYEES

Stefan Asbrede
Valeriya Barysheva
Marion Bauthor
Chiara Bellesi
Andrea Bestel
Alexander Bölk
Yves Boschloos
Cornelia Breda
Armin Conrady
Thomas Fuchs
Britta Fürste
Carlos Garcia Munoz
Nadja Gargulla
Gabriele Gebert
Despoina Gkirti
Stefan Göde
Matthias Grobe
Anna Gromova
Stefan Hack
Andrea Hey
Menglu Jiang
Annette Klittich
Michael Klittich
Martin Kusch
Philip Liepelt
Katrin Majewski
Marco Mattelig
Lukas Mettler
Annika Meyer
Benjamin Neye
Sergej Ponomarev
Marion Porte
Steve Raschke
Muhammed Samer Rida
Saskia Riehl
Volker Röhrs
Thomas Rothe
Florian Rüster
Alexander Schneider
Verena Schönhart
Martina Sievert
Elisa Stellacci
Gerd Strütt
Ludwig Weidner
Anja Weisflog
Yanan Xu
Karen Zaspel

PARTNER / SUBUNTERNEHMEN
LIST OF IMPORTANT PARTNERS

Gisbert Baarmann / Werkstatt für Holzgestaltung
Templin

Büro Christian Meyer
Berlin

Katrin Günther, Professorin für Darstellen und Gestalten
Hochschule Konstanz

ifw / Ingenieurbüro für Wassertechnik
Berlin

Ingenieurbüro Lehmann
Cottbus

Ingenieurbüro Meister
Cottbus

Kersten Kopp Architekten GmbH
Berlin

Kolb Gesellschaft von Architeken mbH
Berlin

planquadrat / Elfers Geskes Krämer PartG mbB
Darmstadt

VIC Planen und Beraten GmbH
Potsdam

Wassertechnik Rostock GmbH & Co.KG
Rostock

ZIMMER.OBST GmbH / Spielraumgestaltung
Spreenhagen

zimmermann + partner architekten BDA
Cottbus

IMPRESSUM / IMPRINT

Fotografien / Photographs
Alle Fotografien von / All photographs by
Hanns Joosten, Berlin
Mit Ausnahme von / With the exeption of
Christo Libuda (Lichtschwärmer), Berlin, S. 190–203

Lektorat / Proof-Reading
Maike Kleihauer (Deutsch / German)
Alison Kirkland (Englisch / English)

Konzept und Texte / Concept and Texts
ts|pk thies schröder planungskommunikation, Berlin

Übersetzung ins Englische / Translation into English
Catherine Johnson-Geskes

Gestaltung und Satz / Design and Setting
Sonja Frank Grafikdesign, Berlin

Lithografie / Lithography
bildpunkt, Berlin

Produktion / Production
HillerMedien, Berlin

Druck und Bindung / Printing and Binding
Grafisches Centrum Cuno, Calbe

Bibliografische Information der Deutschen Nationalbibliothek
Die Deutsche Nationalbibliothek verzeichnet diese Publikation in der Deutschen Nationalbibliografie; detaillierte bibliografische Daten sind im Internet über http://dnb.d-nb.de abrufbar.
Bibliographic information published by the Deutsche Nationalbibliothek
The Deutsche Nationalbibliothek lists this publication in the Deutsche Nationalbibliografie; detailed bibliographic data are available on the Internet at http://dnb.d-nb.de

jovis Verlag GmbH
Kurfürstenstraße 15/16
10785 Berlin

www.jovis.de

jovis-Bücher sind weltweit im ausgewählten Buchhandel erhältlich. Informationen zu unserem internationalen Vertrieb erhalten Sie von Ihrem Buchhändler oder unter www.jovis.de.
jovis books are available worldwide in select bookstores. Please contact your nearest bookseller or visit www.jovis.de for information concerning your local distribution.

ISBN 978-3-86859-548-2